LEGAL BLUEPRINT FOR DEVELOPING AND REGULATING CARBON MARKETS

GUIDANCE FOR LAW AND POLICYMAKERS

JULY 2025

6 ADB Avenue, Mandaluyong City, 1550 Metro Manila, Philippines
Tel +63 2 8632 4444; Fax +63 2 8636 2444
www.adb.org

ISBN 978-92-9277-377-9 (print); 978-92-9277-378-6 (PDF); 978-92-9277-379-3 (e-book)
Publication Stock No. TCS250293-2
DOI: http://dx.doi.org/10.22617/TCS250293-2

Notes:
In this publication, "$" refers to United States dollars.
All photos are by ADB unless otherwise noted.
For easy reference, footnote numbering restarts at the beginning of each chapter. As such, any cross-references within a chapter refer to the corresponding footnotes in that same chapter.

Cover design by Joycelyn B. Lucena.

Printed on recycled paper

CONTENTS

TABLES, FIGURES, AND BOXES

TABLES

FIGURES

BOXES

Lopburi Solar Power Plant. Situated in central Thailand, this plant plays a crucial role in advancing the nation's renewable energy capacity and its commitment to reducing carbon emissions (photo by Ariel Javellana/ADB).

FOREWORD

Carbon markets are increasingly seen as crucial tools for mobilizing finance and driving innovative solutions that boost resilience and economic growth in emerging economies and developing countries. Public finance alone cannot close the massive finance gap, making private sector capital essential. If properly functioning, these markets can play an important role in incentivizing projects that reduce greenhouse gas emissions cost-effectively and provide other benefits, such as improved air and water quality, increased energy access, enhanced agricultural practices, nature restoration, job creation, and community development.

The landscape of carbon markets is evolving and diverse due to the presence of both compliance and voluntary markets. The demand for carbon credits, both at international and domestic levels, is driven by the need to fulfill voluntary climate commitments or to meet compliance requirements established by laws or international agreements.

The international carbon market under Article 6 of the Paris Agreement is gaining traction, especially after the breakthrough at the 29th Conference of the Parties to the United Nations Framework Convention on Climate Change (COP29) with the decision to operationalize the Article 6.4 mechanism. However, carbon transactions under Article 6 are still at very early stages.

The range of options available to countries when they decide to enter carbon markets brings opportunities and challenges. Asian Development Bank (ADB) developing member countries (DMCs) are faced with the task of determining the scope and level of their participation and defining the objectives behind engaging in specific carbon markets. This requires a holistic approach, encompassing both compliance and voluntary markets, and involves complex policy and strategy decisions for ADB DMCs.

In recognition of these challenges, in 2023, ADB published *National Strategies for Carbon Markets Under the Paris Agreement—Making Informed Policy Choices,* which aims to support ADB DMCs in navigating the complexities of devising national strategies for carbon markets under the Paris Agreement.[1]

Building on the 2023 report, this *Legal Blueprint for Developing and Regulating Carbon Markets* aims to serve as a resource for ADB DMCs wishing to design legal and regulatory frameworks to develop and access carbon markets. This is based on the common understanding that clear and effective laws and regulations are crucial to support high-integrity carbon markets and attract carbon finance.

[1] ADB. 2023. *National Strategies for Carbon Markets under the Paris Agreement.*

Since 2019, ADB's **Law and Policy Reform Program**—managed by the Office of the General Counsel—has assisted ADB DMCs with developing legal and regulatory frameworks conducive to establishing carbon markets. Governments have also started putting in place laws and regulations to manage their interactions with carbon markets. Yet many ADB DMCs still lack laws and regulations to govern how actors in the carbon market are permitted to develop carbon crediting projects in their jurisdictions, implement social and environmental safeguards, and monitor and enforce mechanisms to ensure high-integrity carbon project development. Furthermore, ADB DMCs need to define carbon rights and the legal nature of carbon credits in their national laws. Ultimately, clear and robust laws and regulations are essential to enhancing carbon credit quality and providing investment certainty to market participants.

The Asia and Pacific region is at the front line of the effort to drive innovative solutions to adaptation and increased resilience. Communities in this region—especially low-income families—grow more vulnerable every day to the effects of disasters triggered by natural hazards and economic and job dislocation. At the same time, the Asia and Pacific region is a major consumer of fossil fuels—relying on them for a large portion of its energy needs—and emits over half of global carbon dioxide.[2] Consequently, there is a critical need to incentivize and accelerate the development of advanced technologies and solutions to ensure inclusive, resilient, and sustainable growth across Asia and the Pacific.

ADB is committed to supporting the sustainable economic development goals of its DMCs, including through the creation of well-functioning carbon markets. The publication of this legal blueprint is timely for ADB DMCs looking to build their national legal and regulatory frameworks to harness opportunities provided by carbon markets.

I am extremely proud of ADB's Law and Policy Reform Program, which has conceptualized and guided the development of this important publication. I am also grateful to the One ADB team from various departments for their expert inputs, as well as the Pollination team for partnering with ADB to prepare this *Legal Blueprint for Developing and Regulating Carbon Markets.*

Thomas M. Clark
General Counsel
Asian Development Bank

2 *ADB Southeast Asia Development Solutions (SEADS).* 2021. Asia–Pacific Can Still Be Carbon-Neutral by 2050, but Much Needs to Be Done. 1 July.

FOREWORD

Across the globe, developing countries and emerging economies are increasingly recognizing the promise of carbon markets to unlock climate finance, drive low-carbon development, and meet national climate goals. By enabling the creation and exchange of carbon credits—units representing verified greenhouse gas emission (GHG) reductions or removals—carbon markets offer governments a versatile tool to attract finance and accelerate climate action. Through laws and policies, governments can mandate the use of these credits or incentivize their generation to attract both domestic and international investment.

Establishing a domestic carbon crediting framework—including methodologies tailored to national contexts and robust local verification systems—can deliver multiple benefits. Such schemes can bolster national capacity, improve transparency, and ensure alignment with sustainable development priorities. However, they also demand a strong foundation of technical expertise and institutional readiness. As a result, many countries have chosen to draw upon infrastructure established by voluntary carbon markets (VCMs), utilizing internationally recognized carbon crediting standards and registries to scale up carbon credit generation domestically and access climate finance.

Governments must define clear strategic goals for participation to effectively engage in carbon markets. These may include alignment with nationally determined contributions (NDCs), advancing sustainable development, or leveraging carbon finance to strengthen climate-resilient economic growth. A thorough understanding of potential demand sources, market dynamics, and financing opportunities—supported by robust economic analysis—is essential to ensure that carbon market engagement supports broader policy priorities.

Despite clear benefits, designing effective governance structures and policies to guide market participation can be complex. Legal frameworks play a pivotal role in addressing this challenge. Whether a country opts to develop its own crediting system or engage with international mechanisms, a clear and consistent legal foundation is vital. Well-crafted laws can enhance regulatory certainty, foster investor confidence, facilitate cross-border credit transfers, and safeguard the integrity of carbon markets by addressing key issues such as ownership and title to emissions reductions.

Finally, determining where demand for carbon credits will come from—whether via domestic pricing mechanisms like emissions trading schemes, international compliance systems such as the Carbon Offsetting and Reduction Scheme for International Aviation (CORSIA), or the voluntary market—is essential for long-term market viability. While this report does not provide guidance on selecting demand pathways, understanding demand-side dynamics is equally as important for policymakers as creating the conditions for credit supply.

This report offers a blueprint for developing countries seeking to establish or refine the legal infrastructure needed to participate meaningfully in carbon markets. It aims to support governments in laying the groundwork for high-integrity, high-impact engagement that advances climate goals and sustainable development ambitions.

The publication of this blueprint is timely as countries worldwide are embarking on accessing the markets affirmed by the settling of the rules of Article 6 in Baku at COP29, and the countdown to 2030 national climate targets draws ever nearer. Carbon markets will be critical in financing the solutions to meet these targets.

I hope this report will help policymakers enhance their efforts to design and implement legal frameworks to operationalize their carbon market policies as part of their broader climate policy architecture.

Martijn Wilder
CEO and Cofounder
Pollination

ACKNOWLEDGMENTS

This publication, *Legal Blueprint for Developing and Regulating Carbon Markets—Guidance for Law and Policymakers*, has been developed by the Law and Policy Reform Program of the Asian Development Bank (ADB), managed by the Office of the General Counsel (OGC), in partnership with Pollination.

Christina Pak (principal counsel and team leader, Law and Policy Reform Program, OGC, ADB) and **Daniele Quaggiotto** (principal counsel, OGC, ADB) conceptualized and guided the development of this publication under ADB's technical assistance (TA) project *Development of a Legal Framework and Documentation Conducive to Viable Private Sector Renewable Energy and Energy Efficiency Projects.*

Lauren Drake (executive director, Pollination), **Sophie Leitch** (associate director, Pollination), **Joanna Zhou** (executive director, Pollination), **Sarah Denman** (director, Pollination), and **Samim Hoshmand** (associate, Pollination Foundation) conducted the research and produced the initial report, with input from **Marisa Martin** (managing director, Pollination Law LLC) and **Maggie Comstock** (executive director, Pollination Law LLC). The contributions of the Pollination team are greatly appreciated.

This publication also benefited from the technical inputs of ADB experts **Virender Kumar Duggal** (principal climate change specialist, Climate Change and Sustainable Development Department [CCSD]), **Takeshi Miyata** (senior climate change specialist, CCSD), **Euna Shim** (senior markets development advisory specialist, Office of Markets Development and Public–Private Partnership [OMDP]), **Ruchika Saluja** (senior markets development advisory specialist, OMDP), **Gerrit Held** (climate change specialist [public–private partnership], OMDP) and **Maria Cecilia T. Sicangco** (counsel, Law and Policy Reform Team, OGC). Their invaluable contributions are gratefully acknowledged.

Maria Cecilia T. Sicangco, assisted by **Hyacinth E. Rafael-Antonio** (knowledge management specialist [consultant], ADB), led the publication process. Their comprehensive oversight, significant editorial contributions, and dedicated research were vital in successfully completing this publication.

Melanie Kelleher further edited this publication. **Judy T. Yñiguez** handled layout and composition, while **Joycelyn B. Lucena** (IT and multimedia specialist [consultant], ADB) designed the cover. **Maria Theresa Mercado** proofread this publication and **Marjorie Celis** worked on page proof checking. **Rizalyn Ruth S. Aguantia** (legal operations administrator [consultant], ADB) provided efficient administrative assistance during the publication process. **Abigail P. Gotengco** (associate legal operations administrator, OGC, ADB) delivered crucial overall administrative support for the technical assistance. Their diligent inputs are acknowledged and appreciated.

ABBREVIATIONS

ACCU	Australian carbon credit unit
ADB	Asian Development Bank
ANREU	Australian National Registry of Emissions Units
CDM	Clean Development Mechanism
CMA	Conference of the Parties serving as the Meeting of the Parties of the Paris Agreement
COP	UNFCCC Conference of the Parties
CORSIA	Carbon Offsetting and Reduction Scheme for International Aviation
DMCs	developing member countries
FPIC	free, prior, and informed consent
GHG	greenhouse gas
ICVCM	Integrity Council for Voluntary Carbon Markets
IETA	International Emissions Trading Association
ILO	International Labour Organization
IOSCO	International Organization of Securities Commissions
ISDA	International Swaps and Derivatives Association
ITMO	internationally transferred mitigation outcome
MRV	monitoring, reporting, and verification
NEK	*Nilai Ekonomi Karbon* (Economic Value of Carbon)
NDC	nationally determined contribution
PACM	Paris Agreement Crediting Mechanism established under Article 6.4 of the Paris Agreement
REDD+	reducing emissions from deforestation and degradation and the role of conservation, sustainable management of forests, and enhancement of forest carbon stocks in developing countries
SPE-GRK	*Sertifikat Pengurangan Emisi Gas Rumah Kaca* (Indonesia's Certificate of GHG Emissions Reduction)

SRN PPI	*Sistem Registri Nasional Perubahan Iklim* (Indonesia's National Registry System for Climate Change)
UNFCCC	United Nations Framework Convention on Climate Change
UNIDROIT	International Institute for the Unification of Private Law
VCM	voluntary carbon market
VCMI	Voluntary Carbon Markets Integrity Initiative

Mangroves growing along the beach in Kiribati. Mangroves are critical carbon sinks. Their ability to sequester vast amounts of carbon makes them prime candidates for carbon crediting initiatives, driving both environmental protection and sustainable development through carbon finance (photo by Eric Sales/ADB).

EXECUTIVE SUMMARY

In light of the increasing urgency to address climate change and the growing role of carbon markets as a tool for reducing and removing greenhouse gas emissions, many developing countries and emerging economies are seeking to establish or strengthen legal frameworks that enable effective engagement in both voluntary and compliance carbon markets. These frameworks are crucial to ensure environmental integrity, create investor confidence, attract investment, and align with evolving international norms, particularly under Article 6 of the Paris Agreement.

This blueprint is intended to provide policymakers with modular legal building blocks to draw on when designing regulatory frameworks to govern domestic carbon crediting projects and the generation of carbon credits. In this blueprint, such legal frameworks are called "carbon crediting legal frameworks." This blueprint synthesizes international practices, offers practical legal drafting suggestions, and is tailored to meet the diverse needs and capacities of Asian Development Bank (ADB) developing member countries (DMCs). To engage strategically in carbon markets and realize the full potential of finance available, governments should: (i) carefully establish the policy objectives of their engagement with carbon markets, (ii) determine their target source and scale of demand, and (iii) carry out economic analysis to determine how carbon finance can support policy goals and understand the interaction between various carbon market approaches.*

This blueprint is structured into legislative parts that mirror the structure of many legislative instruments. These legislative parts are then broken down into the building blocks and constituent elements to explain key concepts and options for approaches to developing legal frameworks to regulate carbon crediting.

The information has been presented in this way to allow governments to take the building blocks and associated constituent elements and consider how these components could be established within their existing and unique legislative systems. Examples of such adaptation have been provided throughout this blueprint. These examples are intended to provide practical context to the discussion and do not indicate a recommendation for how ADB DMCs should approach these issues, nor are they necessarily a reflection of best practice.

* For further guidance on various options for engaging with carbon markets, see: ADB. 2023. *National Strategies for Carbon Markets under the Paris Agreement*; Voluntary Carbon Market Integrity Initiative (VCMI), United Nations Development Programme (UNDP), and Climate Focus. 2023. *VCM Access Strategy Toolkit*; and D. McLaughlin et al. 2024. *A Ministry Playbook for Corresponding Adjustments: Pricing strategies in carbon markets*.

The key legal issues to be resolved through carbon crediting legal frameworks can be summarized as:

1. **Legal clarity and definitions.** Absent, inconsistent, or vague legal definitions can undermine the clarity and enforceability of carbon market rules. Harmonized definitions (e.g., for terms like "carbon credit," "mitigation outcome," "registry," and "authorization") are needed for both domestic coherence and international compatibility. *Part B, Chapter 1: Introductory Provisions*.
2. **Institutional governance and authority.** Ambiguity in institutional roles can cause overlaps or gaps in responsibility. The legal mandate of governing bodies (e.g., registries, authorization authorities, and monitoring, reporting, and verification entities) must be clearly established through legislation or regulation. *Part B, Chapter 2: Governance*.
3. **Rights over carbon credits and emissions reductions or removals underpinning the carbon credits.** Legal ownership of carbon credits and underlying emissions reductions or removals are often undefined or contested. Land tenure, title, transfer, and usage rights, especially between landowners, project developers, and the state, should be clear to attract carbon finance. *Part B, Chapter 3: Carbon Crediting Projects* and *Part B, Chapter 4: Carbon Credits*.
4. **Authorization for international transfers under Article 6.** Countries and market participants would benefit from clarity on the governance and process for the authorization and transfer of mitigation outcomes. Legal frameworks can set forth the process by which the jurisdiction applies corresponding adjustments and complies with Article 6.2 and 6.4 requirements. *Part B, Chapter 5: Article 6 Requirements*.
5. **Safeguards and benefit-sharing.** Without legal mandates, the protection of rights and distribution of benefits from carbon markets to Indigenous Peoples and local communities may not be equitable. Enforceable legal safeguards, including environmental and social protections, and free, prior, and informed consent (FPIC) requirements, can enshrine the rights of Indigenous Peoples and local communities. *Part B, Chapter 6: Social and Environmental Safeguards*.
6. **Monitoring, reporting, and verification (MRV).** Weak MRV systems can jeopardize environmental integrity and market credibility. Legal enshrinement of robust MRV protocols, independent verification, and data transparency—including, where appropriate, enhancement and enforcement of requirements set by international crediting standards—can give the market more confidence in the integrity of carbon credits. *Part B, Chapter 7: Monitoring and Enforcement*.
7. **Registry systems.** Without a clear legal framework to establish a national carbon registry, there can be uncertainty about its authority, functions, and which entity is responsible for managing it. Countries should utilize informational and transactional registries according to their needs to enhance transparency, confirm the chain of custody, and mitigate the risk of double counting. *Part B, Chapter 4: Carbon Credits* and *Part B, Chapter 5: Article 6 Requirements*.
8. **Enforcement.** Particularly when using international crediting schemes, national authorities may lack powers (or have unclear powers) to investigate, suspend, or revoke project registrations or credit issuances, which can undermine integrity and market confidence. Clear and explicit powers are recommended for national authorities or a designated enforcement body to enforce the requirements of the carbon crediting legal framework, as appropriate within the broader administrative, civil, and criminal legal system in that particular context. *Part B, Chapter 7: Monitoring and Enforcement*.
9. **Transitional and legacy issues.** Newly established carbon crediting frameworks may not automatically include existing carbon crediting projects already registered or issued credits.

Law and policymakers should consider transitional provisions to address issues such as the approach for existing projects under methodologies or standards no longer considered eligible, and ensuring new registries accommodate existing credits while preventing double counting.

A key decision that flows throughout this blueprint is whether a country develops its own domestic carbon crediting scheme (i.e., methodologies created, and credits issued and tracked domestically), or whether it leverages the existing architecture of international carbon markets (i.e., existing independent standards, methodologies and registries) or the Article 6.4 mechanism (e.g., methodologies and registry) to implement carbon crediting projects, create carbon credits, and access carbon finance. Each approach has strengths and weaknesses—as discussed throughout this blueprint—and hybrid options are also available. Summarized in tabular form in Appendix 1 are the minimum requirements for ADB DMCs seeking to establish their domestic carbon crediting scheme and those seeking to use international carbon crediting schemes.

Governments must consider the different options in the context of the broader nationally determined contribution (NDC) targets and plans, the state of existing domestic carbon crediting activities, and the opportunity for scale. Another key consideration is whether to seek opportunities to access strategic sources of carbon credit demand (e.g., voluntary, the Carbon Offsetting and Reduction Scheme for International Aviation [CORSIA], and bilateral trade under Article 6.2). Law and policymakers will also need to evaluate the levels of financial, human, and technical resources and capabilities they wish to invest in domestic carbon crediting governance. This blueprint does not contain guidance on making policy decisions regarding carbon credit demand, but understanding the scale of demand and how to access it is equally as important for ADB DMCs as establishing the conditions for the supply of carbon credits.

ADB and Pollination remain committed to supporting ADB DMCs as they navigate policy and strategic decisions related to developing and engaging in carbon markets, and hope this blueprint can provide some guidance as they embark on establishing legal frameworks to implement carbon market policies.

Aerial view of drilling and well testing stations at the Muara Laboh Geothermal Power Project site, Indonesia. Geothermal projects generate electricity with lower greenhouse gas emissions than fossil fuels and may be eligible for carbon credit generation (photo by Gerhard Jörén/ADB).

PART A: INTRODUCTION AND BACKGROUND

Vehicles on an urban road. Transportation is a significant source of greenhouse gas emissions, contributing to climate change (photo by Derek Lee/Unsplash).

CHAPTER 1

THE EVOLUTION OF CARBON MARKETS

Over the last few decades, market-based approaches and carbon markets have become well-recognized and accepted as pivotal mechanisms to channel financial resources into initiatives combating climate change. Carbon markets are a market-based approach under which carbon credits, representing metric ton(s) of carbon removed or reduced by a carbon crediting project, are generated and thereafter bought and sold by market participants for compliance or voluntary purposes. Countries and regions have utilized these carbon credits to mobilize significant carbon finance and facilitate the adoption of low-carbon and carbon removal technologies and solutions.

The development of international compliance carbon markets was first seen in the early 2000s and was underpinned by the Clean Development Mechanism (CDM), one of the three flexibility mechanisms established by the Kyoto Protocol. Voluntary carbon markets (VCMs) also emerged, developing in parallel with early compliance markets, driven by voluntary corporate demand for carbon credits to offset their emissions. Initially, these two markets did not overlap, but over time, voluntary buyers began to use certified emissions reductions issued under the CDM to offset emissions and achieve their voluntary emissions reduction targets. As of June 2025, the convergence between the compliance and voluntary markets continues to be seen, where certain carbon credits can be used for both purposes.

Many countries have sought to engage with carbon markets in recent years to access carbon finance, despite a rapidly changing and complex policy and market context. For example, since the adoption of the Paris Agreement and subsequent Article 6 Rulebook, there have also been significant carbon market developments toward country alignment to enable Article 6 carbon credits or "internationally transferred mitigation outcomes" (ITMOs) to be issued, authorized, and correspondingly adjusted.

Under Article 6, international cooperation on climate mitigation can be pursued under Article 6.2 or 6.4. Article 6.2 allows countries to bilaterally define the scope and approach for cooperation on ITMOs, but it also mandates the application of standard accounting and reporting rules required under the Paris Agreement. As of 14 July 2025, 100 bilateral agreements had been established between 61 jurisdictions under Article 6.2.[1]

Article 6.4 (also referred to as the Paris Agreement Crediting Mechanism or PACM) utilizes a more centralized approach through the United Nations Framework Convention on Climate Change (UNFCCC) with defined methodologies, but such credits will also be subject to the common

---

1 United Nations Environment Programme, Copenhagen Climate Centre. 2025. *Article 6 Pipeline*.

accounting and reporting rules. The decision at the 29th session of the Conference of the Parties (COP) to the UNFCCC (COP29) in November 2024 by the COP serving as the Meeting of the Parties of the Paris Agreement (CMA) to "take note" of the standards on methodologies and removals adopted by the Article 6.4 Supervisory Body in October 2024 creates a pathway for the operationalization of the PACM. The Article 6.4 Supervisory Body also approved the use of the CDM registry as an interim registry (while the PACM registry is being established),[2] and the first project has now been registered.[3] However, further work is required to finalize guidance and approve methodologies before the mechanism is fully operational. While Article 6.2 is already operational, finalizing these Article 6.4 elements will soon allow countries to engage in Article 6 cooperation under both Article 6.2 and the Article 6.4 mechanism.

Countries can benefit from engaging in carbon markets to finance the reduction of greenhouse gas (GHG) emissions cost-effectively, enhance the economic competitiveness of low-carbon technologies, and generate revenue streams that can be channeled to climate adaptation and resilience. However, to do so, countries looking to transfer ITMOs to international buyers must balance their need to meet their nationally determined contributions (NDCs) under the Paris Agreement with their need for international finance. Countries that choose not to engage with Article 6 may miss out on attracting larger pools of carbon finance, given the expected demand and higher valuation for ITMOs compared to carbon credits that are not authorized and correspondingly adjusted. The 2023 Asian Development Bank (ADB) publication, *National Strategies for Carbon Markets Under the Paris Agreement—Making Informed Policy Choices*, provides further guidance on how national governments can consider key issues to implement Article 6 measures and develop carbon market strategies aligned with national circumstances and priorities.[4]

Demand for carbon credits from voluntary and compliance buyers represents a significant potential source of finance which, with the right regulatory settings, can be channeled into climate mitigation and adaptation efforts in jurisdictions of ADB developing member countries (DMCs). For example, Bloomberg New Energy Finance estimates VCMs globally could reach an annual value of $1.1 trillion by 2050 with the proper integrity safeguards in place. However, this value could be as low as $34 billion if companies cannot trust the quality of credits and financial incentives to buy them are not enhanced.[5]

On the compliance side, the Carbon Offsetting and Reduction Scheme for International Aviation (CORSIA) is expected to become a very large source of demand for carbon credits. MSCI estimates that cumulative demand for credits under CORSIA could reach 137 million tons of carbon dioxide equivalent in Phase I (from 2024 to 2026) and up to 1,299 million tons of carbon dioxide equivalent in Phase II (from 2027 to 2035) in a high-demand scenario. This level of demand could potentially outstrip the supply of CORSIA-eligible credits.[6]

The implementation of VCMs, international compliance markets such as CORSIA, and domestic carbon pricing schemes is anticipated to continue on parallel tracks. However, they are also likely to intersect at key juncture points, particularly as host countries seek to engage with Article 6 mechanisms under the Paris Agreement.

---

2 UNFCCC, Article 6.4 Supervisory Body. 2025. *Meeting report: Fifteenth meeting of the Article 6.4 mechanism Supervisory Body*.

3 UNFCCC. 2025. *Transition of CDM Activities: Programme of Activities: Clean Energy Program Supported by Republic of Korea*.

4 ADB. 2023. *National Strategies for Carbon Markets under the Paris Agreement*.

5 Bloomberg New Energy Finance. 2024. *Long-term Carbon Offsets Outlook 2024: Do or die*. 6 February.

6 MSCI. 2024. *CORSIA: Costs and Implications for the Airline Industry*.

Seedlings at the Ban Pak Ka Organic Agricultural Cluster in Savannakhet Province, Lao People's Democratic Republic. Regenerative agriculture seeks to enhance soil fertility and reduce greenhouse gas emissions by employing practices that minimize soil disturbance and increase biomass. These improvements can be measured for their climate benefits and may qualify for generating carbon credits (photo by Ariel Javellana/ADB).

Theppana Wind Farm, Chaiyaphum Province, Thailand. Wind energy is among the cleanest renewable sources, producing zero direct carbon dioxide emissions during electricity generation (photo by Gerhard Jörén/ADB).

CHAPTER 2

PURPOSE OF THIS BLUEPRINT

This *Legal Blueprint for Developing and Regulating Carbon Markets* presents key legal and policy building blocks to be considered by policymakers when developing legal frameworks to govern domestic carbon crediting. These building blocks form the foundation for developing potential laws and policies and draw out key principles to bolster a country's ability to facilitate high-integrity emissions reduction or removal projects. This, in turn, helps attract finance toward its climate, nature, and sustainable development goals.

Governments have a significant appetite to host carbon crediting projects to incentivize low-carbon development opportunities and attract some of this investment into their country. Project proponents can generate and trade units representing GHG emissions reductions and removals (carbon credits) through carbon market mechanisms. Governments can require polluters to buy such credits or create policies that incentivize their creation and make them available to voluntary and international compliance buyers.[1]

Clear domestic policies and legal frameworks are key to enhancing carbon credit quality, providing investment certainty to market participants, and signaling to the market that a country seeks to attract carbon finance. In this blueprint, legal frameworks for domestic carbon crediting projects and the generation of carbon credits are called "carbon crediting legal frameworks." Carbon finance could fund projects that not only remove or reduce in-country GHG emissions, but also facilitate the transfer of new technologies and skills as local contractors, landowners, and communities are engaged in these projects. If well-designed and implemented, carbon crediting projects can also have multiple additional environmental and social benefits for Indigenous Peoples, local communities, and nature, beyond the climate benefits of GHG emissions reduction or removals.

1 This blueprint is focused primarily on the supply side of the market and does not cover the policy considerations or legal building blocks for countries to create demand for carbon credits, such as compliance carbon pricing mechanisms.

Importance of Developing a Domestic Carbon Market Strategy

To engage strategically in carbon markets and realize the full potential of finance available, governments should: (i) carefully establish the objectives of their participation (such as meeting their NDC commitments and sustainable development goals), (ii) determine their target source of demand and the likely scale of finance available, and (iii) conduct economic analysis to determine how carbon finance can support policy goals and to understand the interaction among various carbon market approaches.[2]

As part of developing a domestic carbon market strategy, ADB DMCs should consider:

(i) Their economic and policy plan for NDC achievement (the development of which should involve cross-government and civil society engagement);
(ii) The potential for emissions reductions and sequestrations beyond the current NDC, as well as sources of finance—including carbon finance—that could be leveraged;
(iii) How carbon crediting fits within the broader policy framework for meeting the NDC, including consideration of domestic carbon pricing and the key sources of investment;
(iv) Sources of demand for carbon credits generated from domestic projects (i.e., international or domestic, and compliance or voluntary sources) and the likely scale of finance from these sources;
(v) If considering engaging in international carbon markets through international cooperative measures under Article 6 of the Paris Agreement:
    (a) the country's strategic objectives to underpin this engagement;
    (b) guiding principles and criteria for mitigation outcomes to be eligible for international transfer, including addressing potential risks of engaging in Article 6 (e.g., "overselling" of ITMOs, which may jeopardize NDC achievement);[3] and
    (c) mechanisms to ensure the government retains some financial benefits for ITMOs, such as through fees or tariffs applied to exports; and
(vi) The systems, processes, institutions, knowledge, skills, and capabilities needed to implement the strategy.

Even with defined objectives, governments can find it challenging to establish strong governance and policies to harness the role of carbon markets to achieve their climate, nature, and Sustainable Development Goals. Therefore, legal frameworks are important in governing interaction with the carbon markets, whether a country develops its own or utilizes international crediting schemes.

Figure 1 summarizes the preparatory steps ADB DMCs should take before developing legal frameworks to access carbon markets.

---

2 For further guidance on various options for engaging with carbon markets, see: ADB. 2023. *National Strategies for Carbon Markets under the Paris Agreement*; Voluntary Carbon Market Integrity Initiative (VCMI), UNDP, and Climate Focus. 2023. *VCM Access Strategy Toolkit*; and D. McLaughlin et al. 2024. *A Ministry Playbook for Corresponding Adjustments: Pricing Strategies in Carbon Markets*.

3 ADB. 2024. *Asia Pacific Climate Report: Catalyzing Finance and Policy Solutions*. p. 154.

Figure 1: Steps for Developing Legal Frameworks for Carbon Crediting and Engagement in Carbon Markets

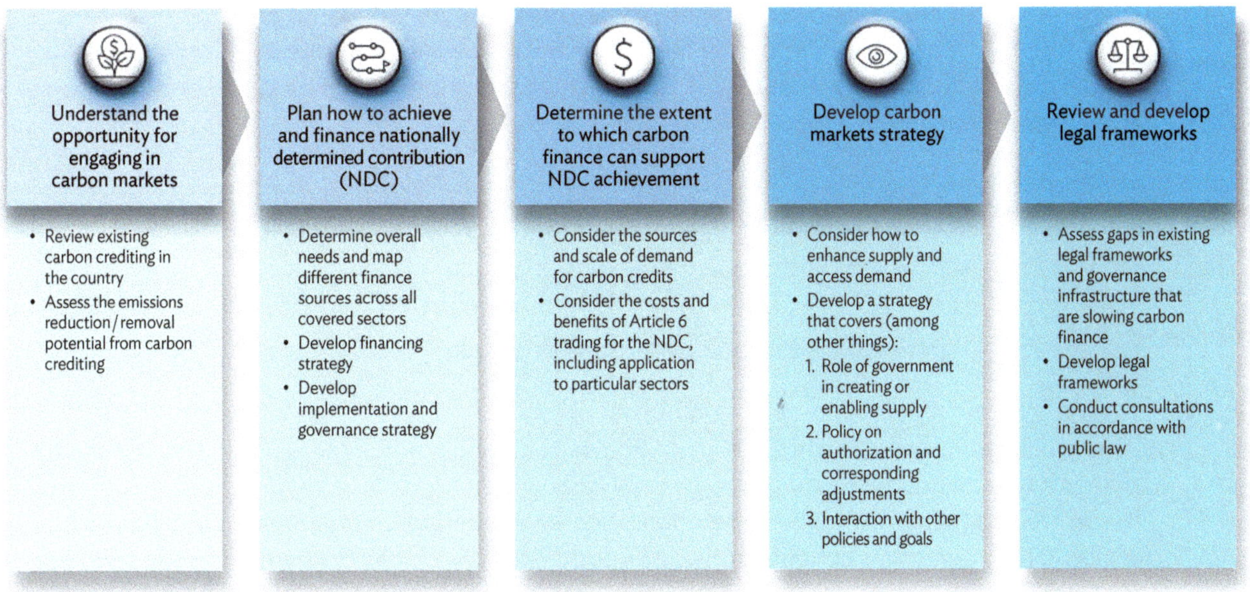

Source: Figure developed for this blueprint by the Asian Development Bank and Pollination.

Benefits of Establishing Domestic Carbon Crediting Legal Frameworks

International carbon crediting standards and registries already provide market participants with an established pathway to develop carbon crediting projects, transact carbon credits, and access carbon finance. However, international carbon markets (particularly VCMs) have evolved in a fragmented and uncoordinated way with inconsistent levels of government oversight and regulation.

Typically, countries have not directly regulated the use of international crediting standards for the domestic generation of carbon credits or their voluntary use. Instead, these standards operate within existing national legal and regulatory frameworks where governments have various legal, policy, and regulatory levers to influence their country's interaction with carbon markets. For carbon markets to effectively channel carbon finance toward countries' NDCs, countries should carefully pull these levers through domestic legal and policy frameworks to create investment certainty and embed high environmental and social integrity. These laws and policies could enable host countries to regulate how carbon market actors develop carbon crediting projects within a host country and facilitate country interaction with Article 6. This, in turn, will help facilitate high-integrity project development from the supply side and increase prices for carbon credits from the demand side.

Robust laws can enhance transparency, establish regulatory consistency across regions, attract inbound private carbon finance, and facilitate cross-border transactions. If well-designed, they can also mitigate market risks for carbon market buyers, such as those concerning the ownership of carbon crediting projects and associated carbon credits.

In recent years, some countries have sought to develop domestic legal frameworks focusing on integration with Article 6 of the Paris Agreement. This has required domestic policy decisions and the development of processes to ensure key principles—such as "no double counting"—and requirements to authorize and report on mitigation outcomes are implemented by both host and buyer countries. As part of this policy approach, many countries have considered how to attract finance from international voluntary and compliance carbon markets to advance their climate and nature policy priorities.

A Key Decision for Policymakers: Developing a Domestic Carbon Crediting Standard or Utilizing Existing International Standards

Some countries have established their own domestic carbon crediting schemes rather than utilizing (or regulating the use of) existing international carbon crediting standards. Developing domestic carbon crediting schemes—where methodologies are created, and credits issued and tracked locally—offers numerous benefits. However, countries establishing their own domestic crediting standards for carbon crediting projects have required deep technical expertise to develop scientifically robust methodologies and set up accounting and transparency mechanisms (e.g., registries and monitoring, reporting, and verification [MRV] obligations).

Many countries and carbon crediting project developers have therefore sought to leverage the VCM and existing independent standards, methodologies, and registries within it to implement carbon crediting projects, create carbon credits, and access carbon finance.[4] For host countries and market participants, it is likely to be more timely and efficient (including from a capability and capacity perspective) to leverage existing international carbon crediting program infrastructure to support the achievement of climate goals, rather than developing domestic carbon crediting mechanisms themselves. Utilizing international carbon crediting standards allows countries to use the established rules and methodologies of these standards, as well as the registries, trading infrastructure, and sources of demand in the voluntary and compliance carbon markets, all of which can take many years to develop domestically.

Countries may also employ a hybrid approach, utilizing aspects of both international and domestic crediting standards as part of their national carbon markets framework. For example, a country could utilize existing methodologies from international crediting standards while also recognizing domestic methodologies. However, this hybrid approach requires significant technical expertise and implementation capacity, as described in this section.

Figure 2 provides a high-level overview of the key decisions ADB DMCs will need to consider when designing their approach to developing legal frameworks for regulating carbon crediting projects and the generation of carbon credits within their jurisdiction. Additional policy considerations will

---

4 The VCM includes standard bodies, voluntary buyers, and carbon credit generators, as well as the trading infrastructure and intermediaries that facilitate the transfer of verified carbon credits to be used for voluntary purposes. Carbon crediting standards "set the requirements for delivering and measuring emissions reductions and removals resulting from a mitigation activity." Footnote 3, p. 153.

Figure 2: Overview of Key Decisions in Designing Legal Frameworks to Regulate Carbon Crediting Projects and Carbon Credit Generation

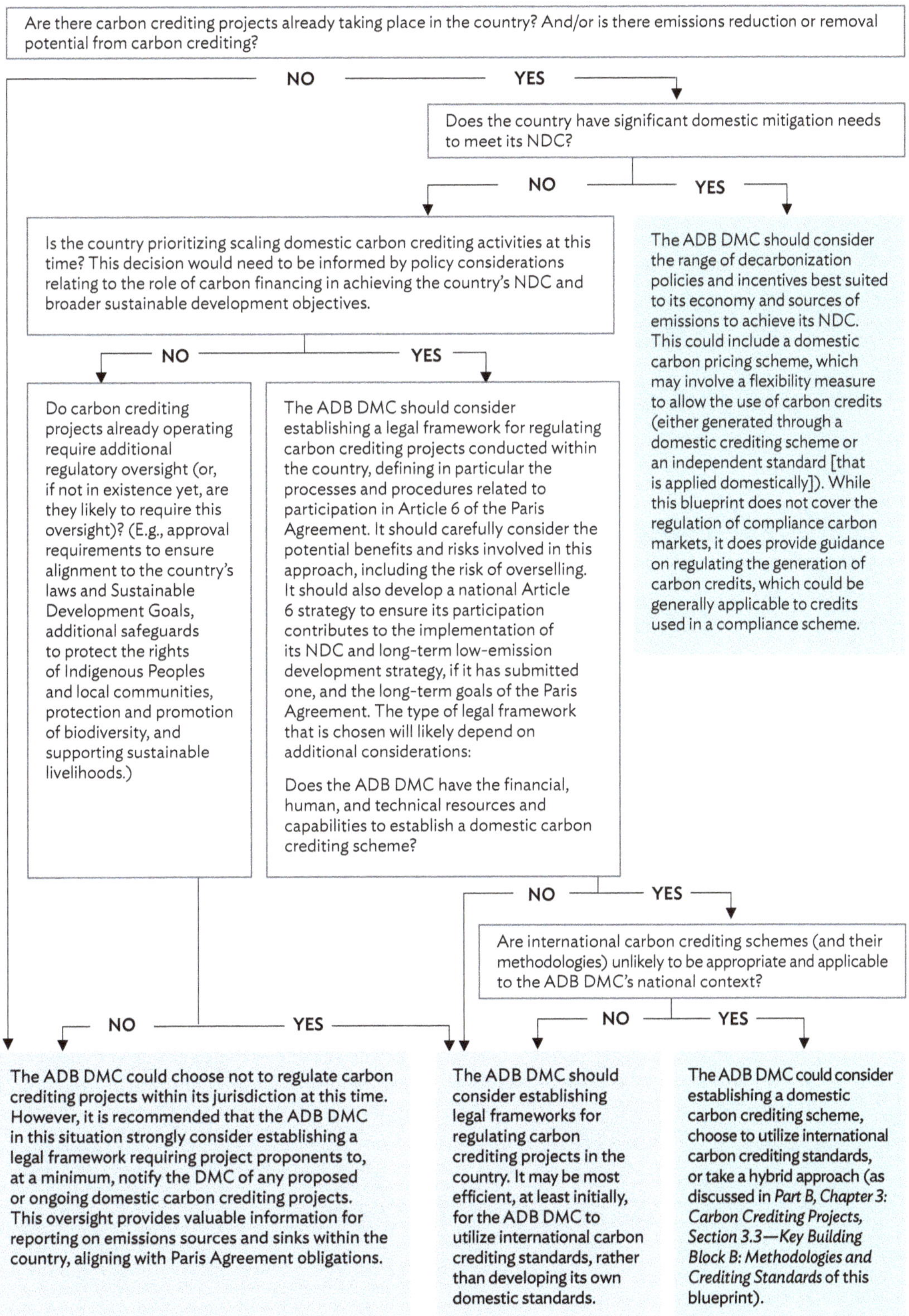

ADB = Asian Development Bank, DMC = developing member country, NDC = nationally determined contribution.
Source: Figure developed for this blueprint by ADB and Pollination.

be relevant in this process, particularly when considering domestic carbon pricing mechanisms, their links to international carbon markets, and Article 6 of the Paris Agreement. The Article 6 Implementation Partnership, the Global Green Growth Institute, the Integrity Council for the Voluntary Carbon Market (ICVCM), the United Nations Development Programme, the Voluntary Carbon Markets Integrity Initiative (VCMI), and the World Bank have published high-level guidance with structured questions to guide the development of national carbon markets strategy. These references serve as a helpful starting point for considering these policy questions in further detail.[5] For Article 6 in particular, the A6 Toolbox—published by the Supporting Preparedness for Article 6 Cooperation program—contains several detailed guides that can assist ADB DMCs in formulating their national carbon markets strategy.[6]

Consideration of Demand

Depending on the regulatory approach taken, carbon credits generated within a country could be used for various purposes, both voluntary and compliance-related. For example, the Carbon Offsetting and Reduction Scheme for International Aviation (CORSIA) allows the use of credits issued by several independent crediting standards in accordance with its Emissions Unit Eligibility Criteria, and is expected to be a large source of demand for carbon credits. Some countries, such as Singapore and Switzerland, also leverage international carbon markets architecture through bilateral Article 6.2 agreements to import eligible carbon credits for their domestic carbon compliance schemes.

Therefore, countries need to carefully consider the source of demand for carbon credits generated domestically. They should assess whether to link this demand to a domestic carbon pricing policy (such as an emissions trading scheme or carbon tax), an international compliance scheme (such as CORSIA), or rely on domestic or international voluntary demand. While this blueprint does not provide guidance on making policy decisions regarding carbon credit demand, understanding its scale and how to access it is equally as important for ADB DMCs as establishing the conditions for the supply of carbon credits.

Aim of This Blueprint and Structure of Content

This blueprint aims to synthesize foundational policy considerations and key legal concepts (presented as "building blocks") for countries to consider when seeking to implement domestic laws to establish a domestic carbon crediting scheme or utilize independent carbon crediting standards in support of their climate and sustainable development policy goals. These key building blocks have been drawn from an analysis of countries that have either implemented domestic carbon crediting schemes or regulated how they interact with international crediting schemes. These building blocks are not an exhaustive list of issues, particularly given the differences in national circumstances and broader legal context, which each country must also consider.

---

5 Article 6 Implementation Partnership, et al. 2024. *Navigating Decisions on Carbon Markets*.

6 Supporting Preparedness for Article 6 Cooperation. *Article 6 Toolbox*.

This blueprint is focused primarily on the supply side of the market and does not cover the policy considerations or legal building blocks for countries seeking to create carbon credit demand, such as through compliance carbon pricing mechanisms (e.g., carbon tax, credit mechanisms, and emissions trading schemes). Therefore, the development of full laws governing interaction with voluntary and compliance carbon markets by ADB DMCs will likely go beyond the core building blocks covered by this document and should be tailored for each country.

This blueprint is structured into legislative parts that reflect the structure commonly found in legislative instruments developed by countries. Each legislative part is further broken down into building blocks and constituent elements to clarify key concepts and present potential approaches that countries may adopt when designing legal frameworks for regulating domestic carbon crediting. Figure 3 illustrates how these legislative parts, building blocks, and constituent elements relate to each other and have been structured in this blueprint.

The information is presented in a way that enables each country to adapt the building blocks and their associated constituent elements to fit within their unique legislative and regulatory systems. For example, the legislative part on carbon crediting projects could contain building blocks covering (i) project proponent requirements, (ii) eligible methodologies and crediting standards, and (iii) integrity considerations. Each of these building blocks could then consist of further detail—for example, project proponent requirements may include constituent elements like character requirements for project proponents.

Throughout this blueprint, examples are provided to illustrate how various countries have considered and implemented the identified building blocks and constituent elements These examples are intended to provide practical context to the discussions within the blueprint. They do not constitute recommendations for how ADB DMCs should approach these issues, nor are they presented as best practice.

Not all building blocks and constituent elements will be relevant to every ADB DMC. Countries aiming to establish their own domestic carbon crediting schemes will face significantly more considerations than those choosing to utilize existing international schemes. These international schemes—such as those developed and administered by nongovernmental organizations like Verra or Gold Standard, as well as the UNFCCC-operated mechanism established under Article 6.4 (PACM)—have their own rules, approved methodologies, and registries. As a result, many of the legislative requirements for operating a carbon crediting scheme are already addressed within these schemes' standards and methodologies. Nonetheless, it can be beneficial for countries to regulate and bring greater control and consistency over how these projects are implemented within their jurisdiction.

Each part of this blueprint includes a summary of the building blocks and constituent elements that represent minimum requirements for ADB DMCs aiming to establish their own domestic carbon crediting scheme, as well as those seeking to use existing international carbon crediting schemes. Table 1 provides an overview of the fundamental building blocks likely to be required for carbon crediting legal frameworks under both scenarios. Appendix 1 offers a consolidated summary of the minimum requirements across all identified building blocks and constituent elements.

Figure 3: Structure of This Blueprint—Legislative Parts, Building Blocks, and Constituent Elements

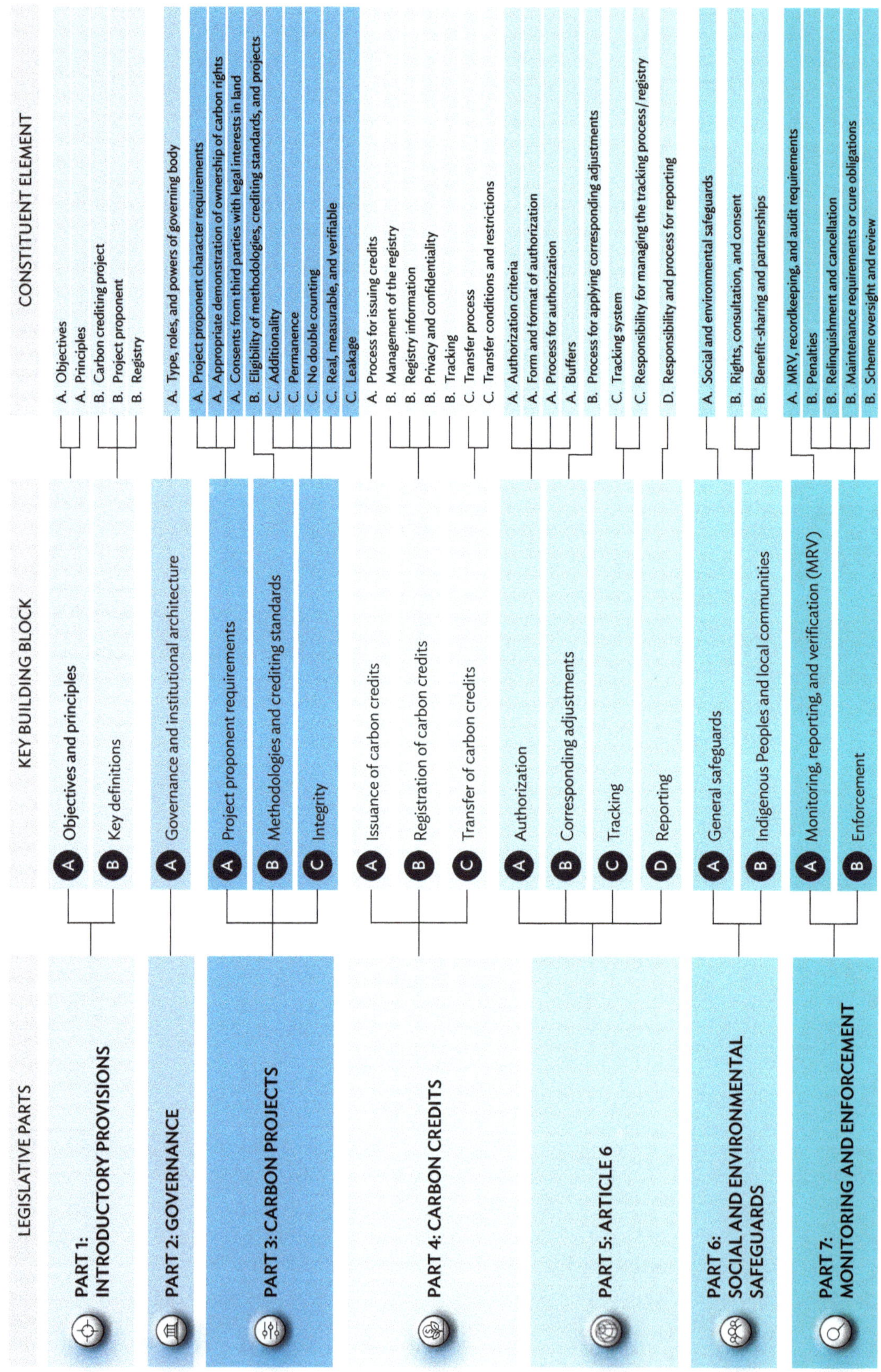

Source: Figure developed for this blueprint by the Asian Development Bank and Pollination.

Table 1: Fundamental Building Blocks Likely to Be Required for Carbon Crediting Legal Frameworks

	FUNDAMENTAL BUILDING BLOCKS LIKELY TO BE REQUIRED		
	Likely Requirements for Both	Additional Likely Requirements for ADB DMC Establishing a Domestic Carbon Crediting Scheme	Additional Likely Requirements for ADB DMC Utilizing International Carbon Crediting Standards
Part 1: Introductory Provisions	✓ Objectives and principles ✓ Key definitions		
Part 2: Governance	✓ Governance and institutional architecture		
Part 3: Carbon Projects	✓ Project proponent requirements ✓ Requirements to ensure that emissions reductions or removals achieved by projects are long-lived, real, measurable, and verified ✓ Requirements to mitigate against the risk of double counting	✓ Process for developing and approving methodologies ✓ Eligibility criteria for carbon crediting projects and a process for assessing and approving projects against these criteria ✓ Requirements for carbon crediting projects to demonstrate additionality ✓ Requirements to mitigate against the risk of leakage	✓ Process for approving international carbon crediting standards (and potentially specific methodologies) that can be used in the country
Part 4: Carbon Credits	✓ Transfer conditions and restrictions	✓ Process for issuing credits ✓ Domestic transactional registry for carbon credits ✓ Process to facilitate transfers, cancellations, and retirements of carbon credits generated under the domestic scheme	✓ Processes for tracking carbon crediting projects and carbon credits generated in the country (most relevant if participating in Article 6)
Part 5: Article 6	✓ Framework for authorizing ITMOs ✓ Process for applying corresponding adjustments ✓ Process for tracking ITMOs that complies with Article 6 rules and guidance ✓ Responsibility and processes for preparing and submitting Article 6-related reports to the UNFCCC		
Part 6: Social and Environmental Safeguards	✓ Social and environmental safeguards ✓ Safeguards relating to Indigenous Peoples and local communities		
Part 7: Monitoring and Enforcement	✓ Enforcement powers	✓ Monitoring, reporting, and verification, recordkeeping and audit requirements ✓ Scheme oversight and review mechanisms	

ADB = Asian Development Bank, DMC = developing member country, ITMO = internationally transferred mitigation outcome, UNFCCC = United Nations Framework Convention on Climate Change.

Source: ADB and Pollination.

A man charges his VinFast electric car in Ha Noi, Viet Nam. ADB's support for VinFast's charging network aims to accelerate electric vehicle adoption and help Viet Nam meet its 2050 net-zero emissions pledge (photo by Viet Tuan/ADB).

PART B:
BUILDING BLOCKS OF A CARBON CREDITING LEGISLATIVE FRAMEWORK

An electric Metrotrans Jakarta bus on the Blok M–Tanah Abang route in Indonesia. In addition to zero tailpipe emissions, electric vehicles are more energy-efficient than gasoline-powered ones (photo by Hilmi Alwan/Unsplash).

CHAPTER 1

INTRODUCTORY PROVISIONS

Introductory provisions in legislation set the scene for context and assist in interpreting and understanding the substantive provisions of the law. The introductory provisions should include a set of objectives, principles, and definitions of the key concepts to facilitate interaction with carbon markets. Figure 4 maps out the building blocks and their respective constituent elements for these introductory provisions.

Figure 4: Introductory Provisions—Building Blocks and Constituent Elements

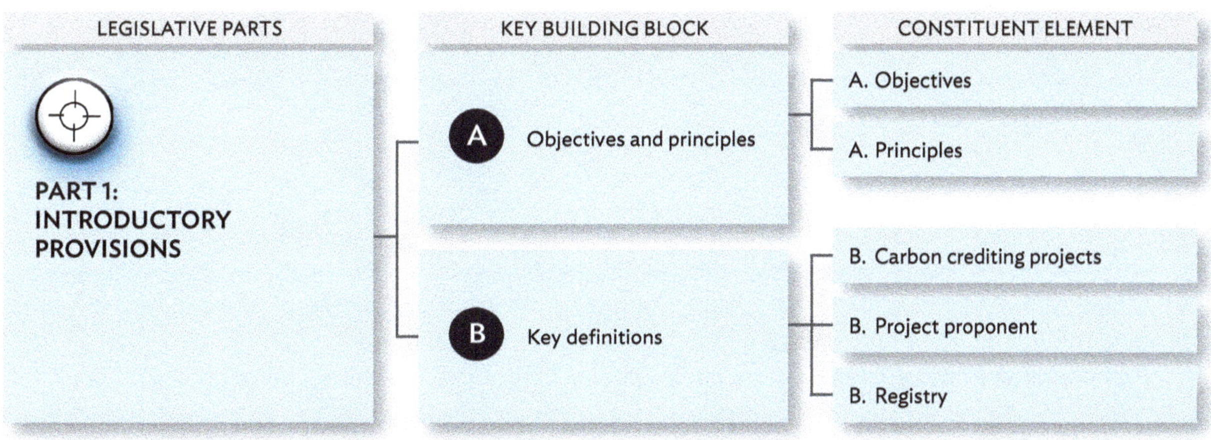

Source: Figure developed for this blueprint by the Asian Development Bank and Pollination.

1.1 Summary of Fundamental Building Blocks Likely to Be Required

Table 2 summarizes the fundamental building blocks for introductory provisions likely to be required by an ADB DMC establishing a domestic carbon crediting scheme and an ADB DMC utilizing international carbon crediting standards.

Table 2: Introductory Provisions—Fundamental Building Blocks Likely to Be Required

FUNDAMENTAL BUILDING BLOCKS LIKELY TO BE REQUIRED	
ADB DMC Establishing a Domestic Carbon Crediting Scheme	**ADB DMC Utilizing International Carbon Crediting Standards**
✓ Objectives and principles. Some of these may be more relevant in the context of an ADB DMC setting up its own domestic carbon crediting scheme, such as those relating to the control and management of carbon projects within the country.	✓ Objectives and principles remain relevant for ADB DMCs seeking to use international carbon crediting standards. They serve to frame the legislation's purpose and can be tailored to reflect the DMC's objectives for regulating the use of international carbon crediting standards within country.
✓ Key definitions, including: - Carbon crediting projects; - Project proponents; and - Registry, which should align with the scheme registry that is established under the legal framework. (See *Part B, Chapter 4: Carbon Credits, Section 4.3—Key Building Block B: Registration of Carbon Credits* of this blueprint).	✓ Key definitions, including: - Carbon crediting projects; - Project proponents; and - Registry, which may include (i) a domestic information registry established under the legal framework, (ii) a registry operated by the UNFCCC (if the ADB DMC primarily engages with international carbon markets for purposes of participating in Article 6 of the Paris Agreement), or (iii) a reference to registries operated by international carbon crediting schemes (including the registry operated by the Article 6.4 Supervisory Body concerning the PACM).

ADB = Asian Development Bank, DMC = developing member country, PACM = Paris Agreement Crediting Mechanism established under Article 6.4 of the Paris Agreement, UNFCCC = United Nations Framework Convention on Climate Change.
Source: ADB and Pollination.

1.2 Key Building Block A: Objectives and Principles

Objectives and principles set out the context for legislation. Objectives typically outline the intended goals of legislation, while principles serve an important symbolic and educational role, guiding the interpretation and application of the law. These principles may be legal, environmental, and/or social in nature and can reflect key international law principles—such as those embodied in the Paris Agreement.

This section identifies potential options for objectives and principles that countries may consider incorporating into carbon crediting legal frameworks. These suggested objectives and principles are commonly found in climate change legislation across various jurisdictions. ADB DMCs should consider including some of these objectives and principles to contextualize the legislation and set a clear direction for its interpretation. Where domestic climate change legislation already exists, ADB DMCs should also consider referencing its objectives and principles. This approach promotes coherence, allows both laws to serve as mutual interpretive tools, and prevents a fragmented approach to overall climate governance.

When deciding whether and how to incorporate objectives and principles into legislation, ADB DMCs should consider the legislation's intended aims and their alignment with the domestic context and circumstances.

ADB DMCs may have different policy aims for their legislation, such as achieving domestic sustainable development priorities, fostering international cooperation, or improving oversight of carbon crediting projects. Depending on an ADB DMC's national circumstances, additional objectives and guiding principles may be appropriate. For example, a DMC with high levels of deforestation could consider including principles that relate to reducing emissions from deforestation and degradation and promoting the role of conservation, sustainable management of forests, and enhancement of forest carbon stocks in developing countries (REDD+). Similarly, if an ADB DMC's population includes Indigenous Peoples and local communities, it may want to consider incorporating objectives and principles specifically concerning their rights.

Box 1 contains some objectives and principles for consideration.

Box 1: Objectives and Principles for Consideration

ADB DMCs seeking to design carbon crediting legal frameworks may consider incorporating the following objectives and principles in their legislation. This list is not exhaustive, and additional objectives and principles may be helpful depending on the individual circumstances of the ADB DMC.

Objectives:

(i) Implementing a country's commitments under the Paris Agreement, including achieving a country's NDC;
(ii) Removing GHGs from the atmosphere and reducing GHG emissions;
(iii) Creating incentives for people to undertake carbon crediting projects within a country;
(iv) Providing for the control and management of carbon credit projects within a country;
(v) Facilitating access to finance, technology, and international collaboration through participating in international carbon markets;
(vi) Facilitating access to carbon finance and foreign direct investment to benefit the local economy;
(vii) Supporting the development and achievement of a country's national biodiversity strategies and action plans under the United Nations Convention on Biological Diversity; and
(viii) Incentivizing low-carbon development.

Principles:

(i) Ensuring integrity through climate change mitigation activities that are transparent, real, measurable, verified, additional, permanent, and not double-counted;
(ii) Recognizing the responsible use of sustainable resources;
(iii) Fostering international cooperation in relation to the financing of climate change mitigation and adaptation measures;
(iv) The precautionary principle;
(v) Recognizing Indigenous Peoples and local communities, their landownership, rights, cultures, customs, traditions, and languages (for ADB DMCs with Indigenous Peoples and local communities within their populations);
(vi) Reducing emissions from deforestation and degradation of forest systems (for ADB DMCs with high levels of deforestation);

continued on next page

Box 1 *continued*

(vii) The principle of integration (i.e., integrating environmental considerations into all relevant decision-making processes);

(viii) The principle of sustainable development;

(ix) The principle of intergenerational equity; and

(x) The polluter pays principle.

ADB = Asian Development Bank, DMC = developing member country, GHG = greenhouse gas, NDC = nationally determined contribution.

Source: ADB and Pollination.

1.3 Key Building Block B: Key Definitions

To enable effective engagement with carbon markets, legislation or regulations should prioritize the definitions of "carbon credit," "carbon crediting project," "project proponent," and "registry," as they are critical components of carbon crediting schemes.

1.3.1 Carbon Crediting Project, Carbon Project, and Project

Carbon crediting projects can either reduce carbon emissions being released into the atmosphere (a reduction) or remove carbon emissions from the atmosphere (a removal).[1] Examples of activities that achieve these benefits include improved forestry management and land use, "blue carbon," waste management, and energy efficiency projects.[2] Additional details on carbon crediting projects and activities are provided in Appendix 2.

Legislation or regulations can define which types of projects or activities undertaken within an ADB DMC qualify as regulated carbon crediting projects. This definition is important, as such projects underpin the generation of carbon credits traded in carbon markets. Additionally, it helps clarify what kinds of projects and/or methodologies are permitted within the country, as well as whether participation in certain international carbon crediting schemes (and standards) is allowed.

1 ICVCM. 2023. *Core Carbon Principles, Assessment Framework and Assessment Procedure*. Revised in May 2024. See Part 5: Definitions. N.B. "Emission avoidance" has not been included here because the concept of avoided emissions is not universally defined by the Intergovernmental Panel on Climate Change (IPCC) or UNFCCC. The prevailing market thinking defines avoided emissions as GHG abatement resulting from activities that are carried out to avoid GHG emissions that would have occurred but for the intervening activity. For example, emission avoidance activities may relate to something that is not a current emissions source but is likely to become one under an alternative, forward-looking scenario (e.g., fossil-fuel extraction) unless an intervention is taken to avoid the potential future emissions. Typically, these activities are not included in carbon crediting schemes, and the eligibility of avoided emissions under Article 6 is not yet agreed.

2 Blue carbon refers to the carbon stored in coastal and marine ecosystems. Blue carbon projects are projects that seek to either reduce carbon emissions or enhance carbon sinks within these ecosystems, e.g., mangrove planting and restoration, wetland and seagrass restoration. International Union for Conservation of Nature. 2017. *Issues Brief: Blue Carbon*.

ADB DMCs could consider the following approaches to defining a "carbon crediting project:"

(i) **Adopting a broad definition.** This could include "projects which remove or reduce one or more GHGs from the atmosphere" or defining projects as "those which comply with a relevant project methodology." Such methodologies can be developed domestically—though this demands high domestic technical capacity—or by international carbon crediting standard schemes. A broader definition ensures all project types are captured and regulated under the framework, offering project developers greater flexibility in the activities they can undertake.

(ii) **Defining by specific project types as appropriate for the domestic context.** These project types must align with the methodologies approved for use (see *Part B, Chapter 3: Carbon Crediting Projects, Section 3.3—Key Building Block B: Methodologies and Crediting Standards* of this blueprint). For example, in jurisdictions with high levels of deforestation, eligible project types could include REDD+, sustainable forest management, afforestation, reforestation, restoration, and/or forest regeneration.

If a country opts to recognize methodologies developed by international carbon crediting schemes, the project type would be determined by applying the methodology. This targeted approach can help ensure that carbon financing is directed toward specific activities identified in their NDC implementation planning as requiring international funding. Some ADB DMCs also address this issue through their Article 6 strategies, defining which project and activity types are eligible for authorization for international transfer (see *Part B, Chapter 5: Article 6 Requirements* of this blueprint).

If ADB DMCs choose to explicitly list which types of projects are allowed, they should consider the pros and cons of each. For example:

(a) Nature-based solutions projects could attract more finance because of rising demand for premium carbon credits, but may require additional safeguards regarding integrity.

(b) Industrial projects could be useful for addressing emissions in hard-to-abate sectors.

(iii) **Specifying exclusions.** ADB DMCs may choose to define which activities are excluded from the scope of "carbon crediting projects." For example, exclusions could refer to projects that fail to meet defined eligibility or integrity requirements under domestic laws or regulations or as required by international standards. Projects could also be excluded if they are likely to cause significant negative effects on other environmental or social outcomes.[3]

(iv) **Including programs as eligible "projects."** Some methodologies, such as those for clean cookstoves, apply to emissions reductions programs rather than site-scale projects. ADB DMCs could consider explicitly including such "programs" within their definition of "carbon crediting projects" (Box 2).

[3] For example, under section 56 of Australia's Carbon Credits (Carbon Farming Initiative) Act 2011, certain project activity types are excluded, including those where there is a material risk that the activity "will have a material adverse impact on one or more of the following: (a) the availability of water; (b) the conservation of biodiversity; (c) employment; (d) the local community; and (e) land access for agricultural production."

Box 2: Carbon Crediting Programs

The concept of carbon crediting "programs" comes from the "program of activities" of the Clean Development Mechanism (CDM), under which project proponents could register "the coordinated implementation of a policy, measure or goal that leads to emission reduction."[a] Once the program of activities is registered, individual project activities could be added without undergoing the complete CDM project cycle.

Similar concepts exist under international carbon crediting standards. For example, it is possible to register "grouped projects" under the Verified Carbon Standard. A grouped project "combines multiple project activity instances into a single, combined project that adds new instances over time."[b]

[a] UNFCCC, CDM. 2025. Programmes of Activities.
[b] Verra. N.d. Grouped Projects.
Source: Asian Development Bank and Pollination.

INTERNATIONAL EXAMPLE

Fiji's Climate Change Act 2021 uses the concept of an "emissions reduction program, project or activity."[a] An emissions reduction is defined as the anthropogenic removal or sequestration of one or more GHGs from the atmosphere or the avoidance or reduction of emissions of one or more GHGs.

There is no limitation on what types of emissions reduction projects, programs, or activities may be undertaken in Fiji, provided that: (i) they meet the definition of an "emissions reduction project, program or activity" (as described in the law); (ii) the project, program or activity is undertaken under an "approved emissions reduction standard" (for example, if declared as approved by the Government of Fiji and/or regulations, international standards like Verra and Gold Standard); and (iii) the climate change director has given consent to that project, program or activity being carried out in Fiji. In giving such consent, the director must be satisfied that, among other things, the project complies with the Act, any regulations made under it, and any relevant policy, guidelines, standards, or procedures adopted by the Government of Fiji, and is consistent with Fiji's NDC. Similarly, the director must approve projects, programs, or activities undertaken in Fiji for purposes of Article 6 of the Paris Agreement. These regulations, policies, guidelines, standards, or procedures may limit the types of projects that the director can approve in either circumstance.

GHG = greenhouse gas, NDC = nationally determined contribution.
Note: While this act has been passed, Part 10 has not yet been gazetted for commencement purposes. It is therefore not in force as of 8 June 2025.
[a] Government of Fiji. 2021. *Climate Change Act 2021*. Sections 2, 4, 11, 14, 46–47, 49–52, 54–57, 59, 61, 63, and 111.
Source: Asian Development Bank and Pollination.

1.3.2 Carbon Credit

A carbon credit is a unit representing an emission reduction or removal of GHGs. These units are "uniquely serialized, issued, tracked, and retired or administratively cancelled by means of an electronic registry operated by an administrative body, such as a carbon-crediting program."[4] Carbon credits can be used for offsetting purposes, among others.

4 Footnote 1, p. 105.

ADB DMCs can take the following approaches when defining “carbon credit” under legislation and/or regulations:

(i) ADB DMCs establishing a domestic carbon crediting scheme should include a definition of the carbon credit issued under the legal framework. This is typically done by reference to the issuance process. The definition may also reference the unit in the ADB DMC’s registry (if establishing such a registry).

(ii) ADB DMCs that seek to regulate the use of independent carbon crediting standards by carbon crediting projects within their jurisdiction may choose to define the term “carbon credit” in addition to “carbon crediting project.” A definition typically includes a reference to the metric underpinning the credit—usually 1 metric ton of carbon dioxide or GHG equivalent—and may also include a reference to those emissions being reduced or removed.

ADB DMCs should also consider clarifying the legal nature of carbon credits in this definition (or elsewhere in their legislation or regulations). Clarity in the allocation of rights to generate, own, transfer, and use carbon credits is vital for carbon markets to function effectively, and core to carbon credit purchaser due diligence.[5] It also provides certainty to project proponents, credit purchasers, and investors regarding how the credits—and their ownership and transfer—will be treated under the legal system.

The legal nature of carbon credits still varies across jurisdictions and legal systems. In many countries, it is not defined in legislation or regulation, leaving market participants and their lawyers to interpret both the nature of the credits and their treatment in the country.

Clarifying the legal nature of carbon credits can also provide greater certainty to market participants about how they can be used, having regard to their legal nature—for example, as collateral in financing arrangements. When determining their approach, ADB DMCs should consider domestic laws relating to such arrangements, including legislative frameworks dealing with the registration and/or prioritization of security interests in property (see, for instance, the international example on Australia in this section). Establishing these linkages can enhance the investment environment for domestic carbon crediting projects and carbon credits by increasing transparency and certainty regarding the ownership and legal interests in carbon credits.

When defining the concept of a “carbon credit” and its legal nature, ADB DMCs should consider:

(i) Domestic property law, in particular, how property and assets are defined under national legal frameworks;

(ii) Domestic laws that regulate or relate to the ownership and transfer of assets (e.g., tax laws, laws on securitization, financial market regulation, contract law, foreign ownership laws, and bankruptcy and insolvency laws); and

(iii) Emerging international definitions and norms.

The International Institute for the Unification of Private Law (UNIDROIT) is undertaking a study of the legal nature of verified carbon credits. This study aims to provide guidance on private law issues concerning the legal nature and definition of carbon credits to support well-functioning carbon markets. The study’s working group has published several draft principles, which offer guidelines that may be useful

[5] ADB. 2023. *National Strategies for Carbon Markets under the Paris Agreement*.

for ADB DMCs considering how to define the legal nature of carbon credits within their jurisdiction.[6] These draft principles also promote clarity and consistency across jurisdictions, which can increase certainty for market participants and, in turn, facilitate the scaling of international carbon markets.

The draft principles from UNDROIT introduce the concept of verification and appears to align with the emerging market view that a carbon credit can be a property right, specifically an intangible asset. While these are helpful guidelines, they are still in draft form. ADB DMCs should continue to monitor the developments in this space and carefully assess the potential implications of adopting any definition for market participants within their jurisdiction.

ADB DMCs should also consider incorporating a reference to the process of "verification" in the definition of a carbon credit. As discussed in *Part B, Chapter 7, Section 7.2—Key Building Block A: Monitoring, Reporting, and Verification* of this blueprint, verification creates greater certainty that the reported emissions reductions or removals have actually been achieved, which is a critical aspect of ensuring integrity in carbon markets. Including the concept of verification in the definition of a carbon credit helps embed this principle into the legislative framework, ensuring that any credits regulated under it must be verified. This should be linked to verification processes and procedures.

This is particularly important for ADB DMCs seeking to create a domestic carbon crediting scheme, as the legislative framework will define the standards for the types of carbon credits that can be generated under the scheme and the quality management processes that support them (including verification). It is also a key consideration for ADB DMCs looking to regulate the use of independent carbon crediting standards, as the legislation can require that any approved or recognized standards incorporate verification requirements and processes.

INTERNATIONAL EXAMPLE

Under the Australian domestic crediting scheme—the Australian Carbon Credit Unit (ACCU) scheme—an ACCU is defined as a unit issued under the relevant section of the Carbon Credits (Carbon Farming Initiative) Act 2011 dealing with issuance.[a] The act also provides that an ACCU constitutes personal property.[b] ACCUs can thus be used as security for a loan or other obligation. They are also classified as "investment instruments" under the Personal Property Securities Act 2009, allowing interests in ACCUs to be registered on the Australian Personal Property Securities Register.[c] Additionally, under the Corporations Act 2001, an ACCU is deemed to be a type of financial product.[d] Consequently, entities involved in issuing, selling, and advising on ACCUs are subject to applicable rules.

[a] Government of Australia. *Australian Carbon Credits (Carbon Farming Initiative) Act 2011 (Cth)*. Section 5.
[b] Footnote a, section 150.
[c] Government of Australia. *Personal Property Securities Act 2009*. Section 10; Government of Australia. *Personal Property Securities Regulations 2010*. Regulation 1.10.
[d] Government of Australia. *Corporations Act 2001 (Cth)*. Section 764(1)(ka).

Source: Asian Development Bank and Pollination.

[6] UNIDROIT. 2025. Draft UNIDROIT Principles on the Legal Nature of Verified Carbon Credits. Note that the principles are still in draft form and are subject to ongoing discussion.

ADB DMCs should also consider including provisions in their legal framework to clarify the legal ownership of carbon credits generated within the country. This can be directly linked to the definition and legal nature of a carbon credit under the framework. For example, in Australia, the registered holder of an Australian Carbon Credit Unit (ACCU) is deemed the legal owner of the unit.[7] The "registered holder" is "the person in whose registry account there is an entry for the ACCU."[8] Clear ownership provisions can enhance certainty and confidence for buyers, investors, and other market participants, thereby creating an enabling environment for carbon crediting transactions.

ADB DMCs that seek to utilize international carbon crediting standards should be aware that the question of legal ownership of carbon credits in this context is an evolving issue internationally. It is closely tied to the legal nature of carbon credits and may involve consideration of private international law principles.

Some countries have adopted an approach whereby all carbon credits generated within their territory are deemed to be owned by the national government. This can give governments greater control over carbon trading and markets within their jurisdiction, while still allowing private sector participation in carbon crediting projects through regulatory mechanisms such as licensing or permitting arrangements. However, this approach may impact carbon finance and investment flows if project developers are unable to monetize the carbon outcomes due to government restrictions, or if the process for obtaining rights to generate and/or sell carbon credits is unclear or difficult to navigate (see *Part B, Chapter 3: Carbon Crediting Projects, Section 3.2.2—Ownership Rights Over Carbon*). ADB DMCs considering this model should carefully assess its potential benefits and risks, along with the policy and legal considerations relevant to their domestic context—including issues related to private property rights.

1.3.3 Project Proponent

A project proponent is generally the entity legally responsible for implementing a carbon crediting project. This may be a single person or multiple people.

Project proponents play a key role in the generation of carbon credits. They are typically responsible for managing the project and its activities, as well as monitoring and reporting on outcomes. They must also be held accountable for any misconduct or compliance issues related to the project.

Laws can formalize the concept of a project proponent, defining it as the person or party that develops a carbon crediting project. A project proponent should be able to demonstrate legal rights to undertake the project and to be issued the carbon credits it generates—either through ownership or a contractual entitlement to the underlying right to the emissions reductions or removals. See *Part B, Chapter 3: Carbon Crediting Projects, Section 3.2.2—Ownership Rights Over Carbon* for further discussion of this concept.

When defining the concept of "project proponent," ADB DMCs should consider the types of individuals and entities likely to participate in carbon markets, as well as the domestic legal structures—such as companies, associations, or trusts—that are best suited to assume the responsibilities typically carried out by proponents.

7 Government of Australia. 2021. *Carbon Credits (Carbon Farming Initiative) Act 2021 (Cth)*. Section 150A.

8 Footnote 7, section 4.

ADB DMCs are encouraged to consider the following when defining who may qualify as a "project proponent:"

(i) The person or entity responsible for carrying out a carbon crediting project. This party should be required to comply with all relevant laws related to project implementation. In some jurisdictions, if a project proponent no longer meets the requirements set out in the definition, they must notify the scheme administrator immediately and may be subject to penalties. *Part B, Chapter 3: Carbon Crediting Projects, Section 3.2—Key Building Block A: Project Proponent Requirements* outlines additional character requirements for project proponents that may also be considered.

(ii) For land-based carbon projects, the party who holds the legal right to the carbon—that is, the exclusive legal right to benefit from carbon reduced or sequestered in trees, vegetation, or, in some cases, soil—and who has obtained the consent of other parties with eligible interests in the relevant land (see *Part B, Chapter 3: Carbon Crediting Projects, Section 3.2.3—Consents from Third Parties with Legal Interests in Land*).

INTERNATIONAL EXAMPLE

In Tanzania, a "project proponent" is an individual or legal entity proposing to implement carbon crediting projects or programs.[a] Proponents must have expertise in carbon trading and financial capability to invest in such projects.[b] Additionally, they must commit to comply with all legal regulations governing the operation of carbon trading initiatives (footnote b).

[a] Government of Tanzania. 2023. *Environmental Management (Control and Management of Carbon Trading Regulations), 2022,* as amended by the *Environmental Management (Control and Management of Carbon Trading) (Amendment) Regulations, 2023.* Regulation 3.

[b] Footnote a, Regulation 23.

Source: Asian Development Bank and Pollination.

1.3.4 Registry

Carbon crediting registries are a critical aspect of carbon credit trading and should be carefully considered by ADB DMCs when developing carbon crediting legal frameworks. *Part B, Chapter 4: Carbon Credits, Section 4.3—Key Building Block B: Registration of Carbon Credits* explores this topic in detail and sets out different design choices regarding the type of registry to be used, as well as its functions and purpose.

Once ADB DMCs have determined the design and function of their registry, these elements should be reflected in the definition of "registry" in the relevant legislation or regulation. This definition should:

(i) Reflect the type of registry chosen, its purpose, and the information it will record. If an ADB DMC decides to establish its own registry under the legal framework, the definition may reference the section that formally establishes the registry.

(ii) Include principles governing the operation of the registry. For example, ADB DMCs could include requirements to ensure accurate, transparent, and efficient accounting of the issuance, holding, transfer, surrender, and cancellation of registry units.

INTERNATIONAL EXAMPLE

Indonesia's carbon markets regulations established a new registry called the National Registry System for Climate Change (*Sistem Registri Nasional Perubahan Iklim* or SRN PPI). The regulations define it as a "web-based data and information management system on actions and resources for Climate Change Mitigation, Climate Change Adaptation, and [the] Economic Value of Carbon (*Nilai Ekonomi Karbon* or NEK) in Indonesia."[a]

[a] Government of Indonesia. 2021. *Regulation of the President of the Republic of Indonesia No. 98 of 2021 on the Implementation of Carbon Pricing to Achieve the Nationally Determined Contribution Target and Control Over Greenhouse Gas Emissions in National Development*. Article 1(14).

Source: Asian Development Bank and Pollination.

The Waste Handling Crane Control Room at the Can Tho Waste-to-Energy Plant in Viet Nam. By converting waste into energy, the facility supports climate action and promotes sustainable waste management (photo by Deng Jia/ADB).

CHAPTER 2

GOVERNANCE

Governance structures are critical to the effective and transparent implementation of carbon crediting legal frameworks. At a minimum, governance provisions should clearly identify the key government bodies involved, define their respective responsibilities, and outline how their decisions are made and/or reviewed (Figure 5).

Figure 5: Governance—Building Blocks and Constituent Elements

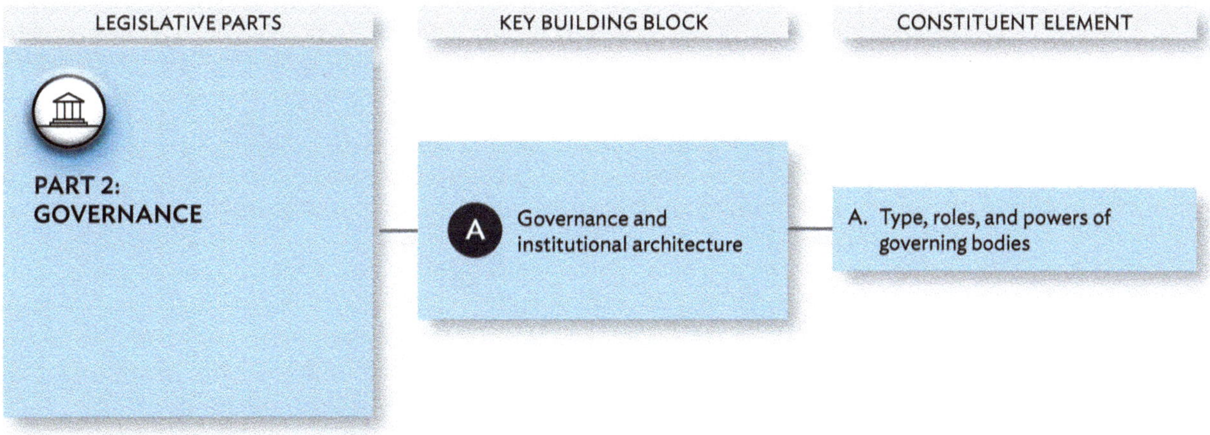

Source: Figure developed for this blueprint by the Asian Development Bank and Pollination.

2.1 Summary of Fundamental Building Blocks Likely to Be Required

Table 3 summarizes the fundamental building blocks for governance provisions likely to be required by an ADB DMC establishing a domestic carbon crediting scheme and an ADB DMC utilizing international carbon crediting standards.

Table 3: Governance Provisions—Fundamental Building Blocks Likely to Be Required

FUNDAMENTAL BUILDING BLOCKS LIKELY TO BE REQUIRED	
ADB DMC Establishing a Domestic Carbon Crediting Scheme	**ADB DMC Utilizing International Carbon Crediting Standards**
✓ Types, roles, and powers of governing bodies, including those referred to in Table 4 of this blueprint (under *Part B, Chapter 2: Governance, Section 2.2—Types, Roles, and Powers of Governing Bodies*). In this context, attention should be given to the resources and technical capacity required to establish a domestic carbon crediting scheme—including the roles and responsibilities that must be fulfilled—as well as to the appropriate level of independence for the designated governing body or bodies.	✓ Types, roles, and powers of governing bodies, including those referred to in Table 4 of this blueprint (under *Part B, Chapter 2: Governance, Section 2.2—Types, Roles, and Powers of Governing Bodies*).

ADB = Asian Development Bank, DMC = developing member country.
Source: ADB and Pollination.

In this blueprint, the legal provisions on governance set out the bodies and structures necessary to facilitate the functioning of domestic carbon crediting projects and the generation of carbon credits. The specific governance arrangements will depend on how the legal framework is structured and the roles assigned to government bodies, which may include oversight, reporting, disclosure, and review functions. Clear and publicly available governance structures are essential to ensuring the efficient operation and integrity of the legal framework, as they enhance both transparency and accountability.

Figure 6 outlines key matters that ADB DMCs should consider when designing governance arrangements in carbon crediting legal frameworks.[1]

Figure 6: Key Governance Considerations for Carbon Crediting Legal Frameworks

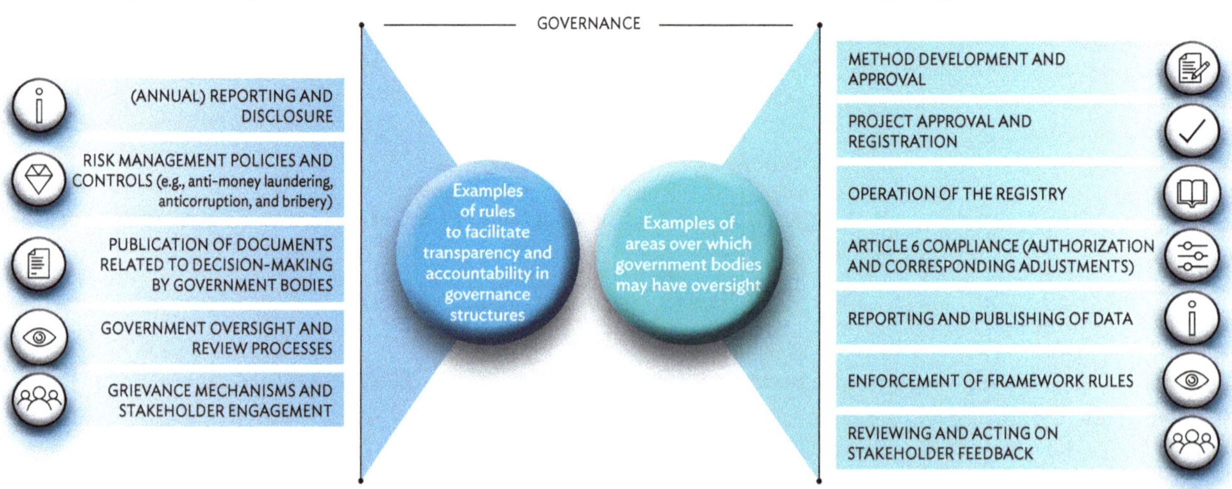

Source: Figure developed for this blueprint by the Asian Development Bank and Pollination.

[1] Depending on domestic capacity, some of the functions set out on the right-hand side of Figure 6 (for example, the development of methodologies and the establishment of a domestic transactional registry) may not be appropriate for a domestic governing body to adopt. Instead, ADB DMCs could consider outsourcing these functions to international crediting schemes.

2.2 Types, Roles, and Powers of Governing Bodies

ADB DMCs may consider various governance structures, including:

(i) Centralizing governance within an independent government body responsible for the administration of the regulatory framework;

(ii) Centralizing governance within a single existing government department—such as one with a mandate for climate change or Article 6-related matters; or

(iii) Adopting a disaggregated model that distributes governance responsibilities across multiple ministries (e.g., through the creation of an interministerial committee) with clear decision-making authority.

An ADB DMC may also choose to adopt a combination of governance approaches. For example, Ghana has implemented a multi-level governance framework to regulate its participation in Article 6 of the Paris Agreement. This same framework also oversees the approval and authorization of carbon credits generated for use in the voluntary carbon market. However, involving multiple government bodies requires significant resource investment and can appear confusing if there is insufficient clarity on how market participants should engage with the system.

The most appropriate governance structure will depend on a country's specific national circumstances, existing government infrastructure, the objectives of the carbon crediting legislation and/or regulations, and the available skills, resources, and capacity to establish and implement new governance arrangements.

A centralized approach offers the benefit of greater clarity and consistency in administering the legal framework and its supporting processes. It can also provide a contact point for project proponents and establish well-defined roles and responsibilities for the regulator or government body, enhancing accountability. This, in turn, can boost confidence among project proponents and other market participants in the scheme.

If adopting a centralized approach, ADB DMCs should incorporate safeguards to preserve the independence of the oversight function and ensure appropriate scheme oversight.[2] They should also establish mechanisms to support effective interministerial coordination by the centralized body, as necessary.

In addition, DMCs should carefully consider whether to establish a dedicated independent government body or to house this function within an existing government department. An independent body can help ensure impartiality in administering the regulatory framework, strengthen specialized expertise and focus, enhance credibility and market confidence, and reduce the risk of regulatory capture. These considerations are especially important for DMCs aiming to develop a domestic carbon crediting scheme.

However, a centralized approach may not be suitable for all ADB DMCs. In cases where financial, human, and technical resources are limited, combining regulatory functions with related government

---

2 See *Part B, Chapter 7: Monitoring and Enforcement, Section 7.3.2—Scheme Oversight and Review Mechanisms* of this blueprint.

activities and functions may offer greater efficiency. In such cases, it is important to implement safeguards that preserve the independence and integrity of the regulatory function. These could include, for example, ring-fencing the regulatory unit from policymaking units or establishing an independent committee to provide advice and recommendations to decision-makers.

Furthermore, a more decentralized approach may be necessary where establishing an independent regulator—or identifying a suitably resourced government department—is not feasible. At a minimum, it is critical to have clear accountability for all functions established in regulations, with sufficient resources allocated to service these responsibilities.

Regardless of the governance model adopted, it is likely that certain functions and powers will need to be spread across different bodies. Even where a new governance body is established, some responsibilities—such as the development of national strategies or the implementation of jurisdictional or programmatic approaches (e.g., REDD+)—may remain with relevant government ministries or departments. For this reason, ADB DMCs should ensure that governance structures operate cohesively, with clear mechanisms for coordination, checks and balances, and inter-ministerial alignment.

Regardless of the approach taken, the roles and powers of the governing body or bodies must be clearly delineated and transparent to support market integrity.

Certain roles and powers will be essential for both a domestic voluntary carbon crediting scheme and interactions with international carbon crediting schemes. Some functions will be particularly relevant when an ADB DMC is focused on developing its own domestic scheme, while others will become critical when the DMC seeks to participate in Article 6 of the Paris Agreement. Table 4 outlines the key roles and responsibilities that ADB DMCs should consider including in their governance frameworks, depending on the specific context.

If a new governing body is deemed necessary, ADB DMCs should consider how it will integrate with existing governance structures. Key considerations include:

(i) Decision-making powers of the governing body, ensuring that any discretionary power is appropriately framed, scoped, and aligned with the responsibilities of the relevant decision-makers within the government;
(ii) Reporting lines, intergovernmental communication, and data linkages with other government bodies and departments; and
(iii) Process efficiency, identifying opportunities to streamline government processes and reduce operational friction, for example, by consolidating relevant functions within a single department.

Transparency and integrity should form the foundation of the governance arrangements underpinning the legal framework for carbon crediting. In designing these arrangements, ADB DMCs should consider:

(i) The appropriate level of independence of the designated governing body—particularly important where the government establishes its own domestic carbon crediting scheme—to ensure impartiality and build market trust; and
(ii) The appropriate level of oversight and reporting to other government institutions, which is essential for reinforcing confidence in the integrity of the policy approach, while also ensuring efficient use of government resources.

Table 4: Roles, Responsibilities, and Functions of Governance Bodies

	Roles and Responsibilities That Will Need to Be Fulfilled	Options for Governance Model
Domestic carbon crediting schemes	• Development of domestic carbon crediting methodologies and methodology determinations. • Review, approval, and registration of carbon crediting projects under approved methodologies, including advice on crediting period extensions. • Maintenance of the domestic registry, including the issuance of carbon credits to registered projects with verified emissions reductions and/or removals, and the processing of transfer, cancellation, and retirement requests from account holders. • Oversight of projects, including the review of project reports and enforcement of compliance in cases of breach. • Provision of a mechanism for grievance resolution. • Organization of educational programs on carbon crediting projects and carbon markets. • Reporting to ministers on the effectiveness of the scheme in achieving its objectives.	ADB DMCs that establish their own domestic carbon crediting scheme for the voluntary carbon market will likely need to create an independent government body—such as a regulator—to administer the scheme. This is due to the significant administrative burden and the specialized expertise required to operate a domestic crediting system effectively. Ensuring separation and independence between the policymaking department and the scheme administrator can help build public confidence in the objectivity and impartiality of decisions and foster greater trust in the market. Alternatively, ADB DMCs may choose to administer the scheme within existing government departments. In such cases, careful consideration must be given to the department's resources and capacity to undertake these responsibilities, as well as to any potential concerns regarding independence and integrity (e.g., if the government also participates in carbon crediting projects or is purchasing domestic credits for its own use).
Regulation of international carbon crediting schemes	• Review and—if desired by the ADB DMC—approval of carbon crediting projects conducted under international carbon crediting schemes within the ADB DMC's jurisdiction. This approval may include applying additional integrity requirements beyond those required by the international carbon crediting standard (e.g., assessing methodology suitability, alignment with the DMC's sustainable development goals, and the project's proposed engagement with landowners and Indigenous Peoples and local communities). • Review of project reporting to ensure compliance with national laws and regulations. • Organization of educational programs on carbon crediting projects and carbon markets.	Given the comparatively lower administrative burden in this regulatory context, it will likely be sufficient for an ADB DMC to assign these functions to an existing government department.

continued on next page

Table 4 *continued*

	ROLES AND RESPONSIBILITIES THAT WILL NEED TO BE FULFILLED	OPTIONS FOR GOVERNANCE MODEL
	• Reporting to ministers on the effectiveness of the scheme in achieving its objectives. • Liaison with international crediting schemes, as required—for example, where host country advice is needed under international crediting standards to extend crediting periods.	
Participating in Article 6	• Policy and strategy direction for Article 6 participation, including decisions on eligible activities for authorization. • Authorization of public or private entities to participate as activity participants under the Article 6.4 mechanism. • Approval of activities that participants can use in the country under the Article 6.4 mechanism. • Review of applications and issuance of authorizations for international transfers of carbon credits. • Authorization of cooperative approaches and entities for purposes of Article 6.2, as applicable. • Provision of a mechanism for grievance resolution. • Tracking of incoming and outgoing ITMOs. • Application of corresponding adjustments in respect of incoming and outgoing ITMOs. • Preparation of annual and regular reports required for participation in Article 6. • Reporting to other government departments on the impact of ITMO transfers on sectoral NDC plans.	Countries seeking to participate in Article 6 often adopt a multi-faceted governance approach to ensure effective intersectoral coordination, along with appropriate oversight and strategic direction from senior levels of government. This is important, as Article 6 participation can impact a country's ability to meet its climate targets across various NDC sectors. This may, for example, entail: • Oversight and strategic policy direction from senior levels of government, such as through a ministry or an inter-ministerial committee. • Establishment of a technical committee to assess the technical aspects of Article 6 participation—such as reviewing specific activities and methodologies under the Article 6.4 mechanism—and to provide recommendations to government decision-makers. • Centralization of administrative aspects of Article 6 participation within a single body or department. This could include engagement with project proponents (e.g., receiving and reviewing applications for authorization and issuing letters of authorization), administering the Article 6 tracking system, preparing Article 6 reports, and applying corresponding adjustments. Certain functions—particularly reporting and the application of corresponding adjustments—may be assigned to departments already responsible for the ADB DMC's engagement with the CDM and broader Paris Agreement reporting, including the preparation of the national greenhouse gas inventory.

ADB = Asian Development Bank, Article 6 = Article 6 of the Paris Agreement, CDM = Clean Development Mechanism, DMC = developing member country, GHG = greenhouse gas, ITMO = internationally transferred mitigation outcome, NDC = nationally determined contribution.

Source: ADB and Pollination.

INTERNATIONAL EXAMPLE

In Tanzania, the regulatory framework follows a semi-centralized approach that cascades from the minister responsible for the environment and involves various line ministries and government entities, as illustrated in the figure below.

Tanzania's Carbon Markets Governance Framework

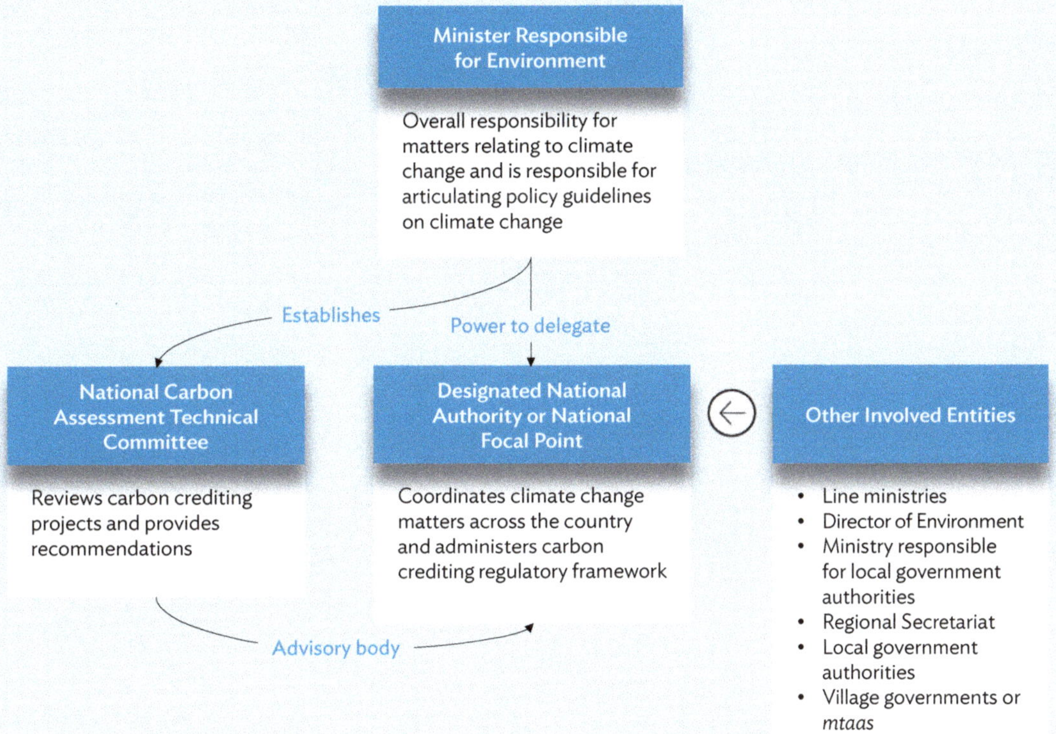

Source: Figure developed for this blueprint by the Asian Development Bank and Pollination.

Under the regulations, the minister is responsible for climate change matters and articulating policy guidelines, including carbon trading.[a] The minister may delegate this authority to the designated national authority or the national focal point (defined as the ministry designated under the regulations to coordinate matters relating to environment and carbon trading projects in Tanzania).

The designated national authority or national focal point is responsible for coordinating climate change-related matters across Tanzania, linking the country with international processes for climate change, providing policy guidance on carbon markets and other crediting mechanisms, and performing core functions under the regulatory framework, among other responsibilities.

The regulations also require the ministry responsible for the environment to establish a National Carbon Project Assessment Technical Committee to serve as an advisory body to the designated national authority or national focal point. This committee is chaired by the director of environment.

In addition, sector ministries are assigned several roles, including:

- providing sector technical, administrative, and legal advice on carbon crediting projects;
- issuing clearance letters for projects proposed within their respective sectors;

continued on next page

International Example *continued*

- recognizing "certified carbon emission reduction units" from sector-specific carbon crediting projects in the national GHG inventory;
- identifying and mapping potential areas for carbon trading mechanisms; and
- monitoring and evaluating carbon trading mechanisms and submitting reports to the designated national authority or national focal point.[b]

The regulations also set out the functions and roles of the director of environment, the ministry responsible for local government authorities, the regional secretariat, local government authorities, and village governments or mtaas.

GHG = greenhouse gas.

[a] Government of Tanzania. 2023. *The Environmental Management (Control and Management of Carbon Trading) Regulations, 2022*, as amended by *The Environmental Management (Control and Management of Carbon Trading) (Amendment) Regulations, 2023*. Regulation 6(1).

[b] Footnote a, Regulations 9, 11, 12, and 14.

Source: Asian Development Bank and Pollination.

A dense bamboo forest in Kyoto, Japan. Afforestation and reforestation efforts contribute to carbon sequestration while also delivering co-benefits such as biodiversity enhancement, erosion control, and improved ecosystem resilience for surrounding communities (photo by Cam Stockdale/Unsplash).

Kali Gandaki Dam, Nepal. Hydropower—the use of flowing water for energy—has been harnessed for thousands of years for mechanical tasks. Today, the Kali Gandaki "A" Hydroelectric Power Station generates electricity from the Kali Gandaki River, contributing to renewable energy development in Nepal (photo by Samir Jung Thapa/ADB).

CHAPTER 3

CARBON CREDITING PROJECTS

Specific requirements for conducting carbon crediting projects are essential to ensure the effective operation of high-integrity carbon markets and to build investor confidence. At a minimum, these requirements should address how projects are approved, which standards or methodologies may be used, and what measures are in place to uphold the integrity of carbon crediting projects (Figure 7).

Figure 7: Carbon Crediting Projects—Building Blocks and Constituent Elements

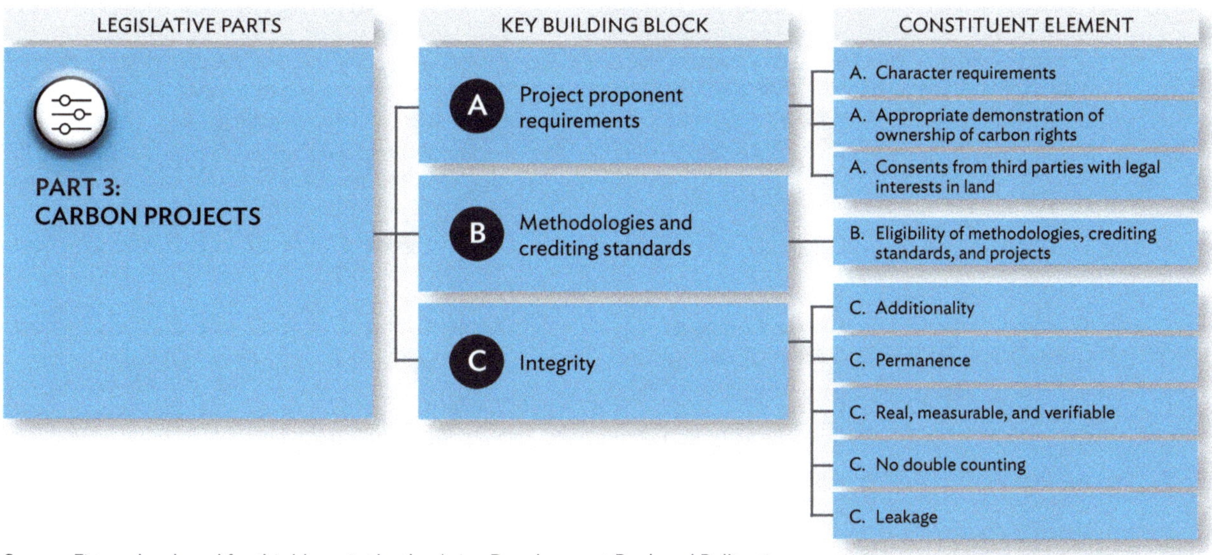

Source: Figure developed for this blueprint by the Asian Development Bank and Pollination.

3.1 Summary of Fundamental Building Blocks Likely to Be Required

Table 5 summarizes the key building blocks likely required for provisions setting out the requirements for conducting carbon crediting projects in ADB DMCs, using both domestic carbon crediting schemes and international carbon crediting standards.

Table 5: Specific Requirements for Carbon Crediting Projects—Fundamental Building Blocks Likely to Be Required

<table>
<tr><th colspan="2">FUNDAMENTAL BUILDING BLOCKS LIKELY TO BE REQUIRED</th></tr>
<tr><th>ADB DMC Establishing a Domestic Carbon Crediting Scheme</th><th>ADB DMC Utilizing International Carbon Crediting Standards</th></tr>
<tr><td>✓ Project proponent requirements, including:
- Character requirements (e.g., Know-Your-Customer requirements);
- Appropriate demonstration of ownership of carbon rights; and
- Consents from third parties with legal interests in land.</td><td>✓ Project proponent requirements, including:
- Character requirements (e.g., Know-Your-Customer requirements);
- Appropriate demonstration of ownership of carbon rights; and
- Consents from third parties with legal interests in land.
While international carbon crediting schemes will address these elements, including them in national legal frameworks can help support domestic enforceability of these requirements and safeguard the rights of those involved in or impacted by carbon crediting projects.</td></tr>
<tr><td>✓ A process for developing and approving project methodologies (including ensuring that these align with integrity principles set out in Part B, Chapter 3: Carbon Crediting Projects, Section 3.4—Key Building Block C: Approach to Managing Integrity of this blueprint).</td><td>? Methodologies are approved under the rules of the international carbon crediting mechanisms. However, ADB DMCs may choose to specify which of these methodologies are approved for use in the country—for example, by maintaining a regularly updated list of pre-approved methodologies.
Note: ADB DMCs wishing to participate in the PACM must establish a process for determining and notifying the Article 6.4 Supervisory Body of the types of Article 6, paragraph 4 activities (A6.4 activities) they will approve for use within their country.</td></tr>
<tr><td>? In addition to the domestic scheme established by their legal framework, ADB DMCs may also approve international carbon crediting standards for use within their country.</td><td>✓ A process for approving international carbon crediting standards for use in the country, including, where applicable, processes to facilitate participation in the PACM.</td></tr>
<tr><td>✓ Eligibility criteria for carbon crediting projects, along with a process for assessing and approving projects based on these criteria.</td><td>? Eligibility criteria are not required, as they are usually addressed in the rules of the international carbon crediting scheme and its methodologies.
However, ADB DMCs may choose to establish an approval process for domestic carbon crediting projects that would apply additional integrity criteria, safeguards, and/or project requirements that align with national policy priorities and sustainable development goals. This approval would be separate from, and in addition to, the approval and registration process conducted by the international carbon crediting scheme's administrator.
ADB DMCs seeking to participate in Article 6 must consider a process for authorizing projects, which involves assessing projects at the individual level and considering any additional eligibility requirements (see Part B, Chapter 5: Article 6 Requirements, Section 5.2—Key Building Block A: Authorization).</td></tr>
</table>

continued on next page

Table 5 *continued*

FUNDAMENTAL BUILDING BLOCKS LIKELY TO BE REQUIRED	
ADB DMC Establishing a Domestic Carbon Crediting Scheme	**ADB DMC Utilizing International Carbon Crediting Standards**
✓ Requirements for carbon crediting projects to demonstrate additionality.[a]	? Requirements for additionality are not necessary, as this matter is already addressed under the international crediting standard. However, ADB DMCs intending to use international crediting standards should ensure that any standard approved for use in the country includes its own additionality requirement. Moreover—or as an alternative—ADB DMCs may include a broad provision in their laws and/or regulations stating that all approved projects must demonstrate additionality.
✓ Requirements to ensure the permanence of emissions reductions or removals achieved by carbon crediting projects.	✓ The ADB DMC should be able to enforce the permanence obligation established by an international crediting standard.
✓ Requirements to mitigate the risk of double counting.	✓ Requirements to mitigate the risk of double counting, particularly if the ADB DMC seeks to engage in Article 6 of the Paris Agreement. These requirements must be reflected in the DMC's rules on authorization and corresponding adjustments.
✓ Requirements to ensure that emissions reductions and removals generated under the scheme are real, measurable, and verified.	✓ Requirements to ensure that emissions reductions and removals generated by carbon crediting projects undertaken in the ADB DMC's jurisdiction are real, measurable, and verified—for example, by ensuring that any international carbon crediting standard approved for use in the country has provisions to uphold this integrity principle.
✓ Requirements to mitigate the risk of leakage.[b]	✗ ADB DMCs may consider including a general requirement related to leakage to enhance the integrity of their legislative framework. However, leakage is typically addressed in the rules and methodologies of international carbon crediting schemes.

ADB = Asian Development Bank, DMC = developing member country, PACM = Paris Agreement Crediting Mechanism established under Article 6.4 of the Paris Agreement.

Legend: ✓ likely to be required.
? not likely to be required but with details for determination.
✗ not likely to be required.

[a] "Emission reductions or removals from a mitigation activity are additional if the mitigation activity would not have taken place in the absence of the added incentive created by the carbon offsets." World Wildlife Fund (WWF-US) et al. 2022. Methodology for Assessing the Quality of Carbon Credits. p. 4.

[b] Leakage is defined as "the net change of GHG emissions or removals that are attributable to the mitigation activity [for a project] but occur outside the boundary of that [project]." Footnote a, p. 5.

Source: ADB and Pollination.

3.2 Key Building Block A: Project Proponent Requirements

Proponent requirements in carbon market legal frameworks serve as safeguards by screening project proponents prior to project registration and approval, and by imposing ongoing standards for their conduct. These requirements help uphold the integrity of carbon markets and credit-generating projects, while also mitigating the risk of negative impacts associated with such projects.

Project proponent requirements fall into three broad categories: character, ownership of carbon rights, and consent from other rights holders. These requirements help ensure the integrity of carbon projects and enhance investor confidence by ensuring that project proponents possess the necessary expertise and capacity to implement the project, and that they hold the legal rights and arrangements needed with relevant stakeholders.

These legislative provisions can be included whether an ADB DMC is establishing its own domestic carbon crediting scheme or adding an additional layer of protection to complement the requirements of adopted international carbon standards.

These legislative provisions are relevant for "projects," "programs of activities," or "grouped projects." In the case of "programs of activities" or "grouped projects," proponent requirements should be established for the proponent of the entire program or grouped project, rather than each time a new activity is registered.[1] Additionally, land-related considerations may be less relevant if the aggregated projects do not occur on, or relate to, a specific area of land.

3.2.1 Character Requirements

Mandating that project proponents meet robust character standards can enhance the integrity of carbon crediting projects. These requirements also help safeguard against illegal conduct, such as fraud.

ADB DMCs may consider including the following project proponent character requirements:

(i) **Compliance with Know-Your-Customer (KYC) requirements** to prevent fraud and reduce financial risks (e.g., money laundering and terrorist financing), including identity verification, proof of domicile, evidence of corporate good standing, and valid business licenses;

(ii) **Avoidance of false, misleading, or otherwise improper conduct**, including in interactions with landowners and other rights holders;

(iii) **Provision of contract terms that are accessible, fair, and appropriate** to the specific context;

(iv) **Establishment of appropriate benefit-sharing mechanisms**, such as prompt and reliable distribution of funds;

(v) **No history of bankruptcy, criminal convictions, or fraudulent conduct**; and

(vi) **Maintenance of robust internal systems** to support effective reporting, monitoring, and recordkeeping.

---

[1] See *Part B, Chapter 1: Introductory Provisions, Section 1.3.1—Carbon Crediting Project, Carbon Project, and Project* of this blueprint.

ADB DMCs may align these character requirements with existing regulatory character standards, such as those set out in company registration laws, credit laws, and general "doing business" requirements.

3.2.2 Ownership Rights Over Carbon

"Carbon rights" refer to the legal entitlement to the benefits arising from the reduction and/or sequestration of GHG emissions resulting from activities carried out under a carbon project. It is important to distinguish the legal right to the underlying GHG emissions reduction or removal from the ownership of the carbon credit itself, which is a tradable asset representing 1 metric ton of verified carbon dioxide equivalent removed or reduced (see *Part B, Chapter 1: Introductory Provisions, Section 1.3.2—Carbon Credit* of this blueprint).[2]

The legal nature of the underlying rights to GHG emissions reductions or removals, and how these rights can be held and transferred, will depend on each country's domestic law. Most countries do not have explicit legislation addressing carbon rights; however, existing laws such as property law, constitutional provisions, and forestry statutes may be relevant and should be carefully examined. For example, in Australia, rights to carbon sequestered from forests are governed by state law: some states classify these rights as a common law *profit à prendre* ("profit to be taken"), while others define them as a statutory property interest.[3] If ADB DMCs seek to clarify how carbon rights are owned, transferred, or registered, these broader legal contexts will need to be considered. Clear legal frameworks that establish how project proponents can obtain, own, and transfer carbon rights support market transparency and help mitigate risks related to a buyer's ability to secure legal title to the resulting carbon credits.

To improve clarity and transparency, ADB DMCs should consider including, within carbon crediting legal frameworks, provisions that clarify legal ownership of carbon rights, identify who holds the legal authority to transfer rights arising from emissions reductions or removals, and outline how ownership of carbon rights can be recorded in public registers. For example, ADB DMCs could introduce the concept of a registrable "carbon sequestration property right" for land-based projects. The registered holder of this right would have the exclusive and distinct statutory legal right to the carbon sequestered and/or carbon stocks associated with a carbon crediting project on the specific parcel of land to which the right applies.

One area where legislative clarity may assist market participants is in determining whether ownership of carbon rights (as distinct from ownership of the *carbon credit itself*) can be made subject to other ownership interests—for example, to enable their use as collateral for loans. Whether this is appropriate will depend on the legal nature of carbon rights in the jurisdiction and the broader legal framework governing security interests. The rights of landowners and other parties with legal interests

---

2 The draft UNIDROIT principles on the legal nature of verified carbon credits do not include principles relating to carbon rights as defined in this section. These draft principles focus on the definition of carbon credits as the end tradeable asset. See UNIDROIT. 2025. Draft UNIDROIT Principles on the Legal Nature of Verified Carbon Credits.

3 "A *profit à prendre* is a right to take from the land owned by another person part of the natural produce grown on that land or part of the soil, earth or rock comprising the land. Like an easement, a profit à prendre may be enjoyed as a benefit to other land or it may exist in gross (i.e., without having a dominant tenement). [...] Examples of profit à prendres include rights to graze stock; plant and harvest crops; quarry stone, sand, or gravel; or take timber." New South Wales Land Registry Services. Profit à Prendre.

in land must also be carefully considered.[4] Regardless of the approach adopted, ADB DMCs should provide clear rules on these issues to ensure that carbon markets operate with integrity and efficiency.

Where the law provides that carbon rights are owned by a person or entity other than the project proponent, the project proponent would typically enter into a contract with that party to obtain those rights. The legal framework could also require the project proponent to carry out a free, prior, and informed consent (FPIC) process,[5] as well as establish a benefit-sharing or equity-sharing arrangement with the landowner.[6]

INTERNATIONAL EXAMPLE

Fiji's Climate Change Act 2021 clarifies that, when a carbon sequestration property right is registered in accordance with the act, the right holder is entitled to "deal with the right whether by sale, transfer, mortgage, charge or pledge."[a]

[a] Government of Fiji. 2021. *Climate Change Act 2021.* Section 45(2)(f).
Source: Asian Development Bank and Pollination.

3.2.3 Consents from Third Parties with Legal Interests in Land

As discussed in *Part A: Introduction and Background* of this blueprint, carbon crediting projects can deliver a range of domestic benefits and should be designed to maximize positive outcomes for climate, nature, and people. In particular, such projects can create income streams that support sustainable livelihoods and facilitate the transition to a low-carbon economy. To realize these benefits, project proponents must engage all individuals and groups who are involved in or materially affected by the project. This includes those with legal or customary rights to the land, as well as those actively engaged in its stewardship, such as Indigenous Peoples and local communities. ADB DMCs should ensure that the rights and protections of these groups, under both international and domestic law, are appropriately safeguarded.[7] In addition, consents may be required from other parties with legal or beneficial interests in the land, such as mortgagees.

Involving landowners, rights holders, and stewards in carbon crediting projects is also critical to maintaining the integrity and durability of the climate outcomes achieved. Carbon crediting standards typically require project proponents to ensure the permanence of mitigation outcomes.[8] This often means that certain activities cannot be undertaken on the land during the permanence period to prevent reversal of emissions reductions or removals, and that periodic maintenance of the land may be necessary. When landowners and rights holders are engaged as active partners from the outset,

[4] See *Part B, Chapter 3: Carbon Crediting Projects, Section 3.2.3—Consents from Third Parties with Legal Interests in Land* of this blueprint.

[5] See *Part B, Chapter 3: Carbon Crediting Projects, Section 3.2.3—Consents from Third Parties with Legal Interests in Land* and *Part B, Chapter 6: Social and Environmental Safeguards, Section 6.3.1—Rights, Consultation, and Consent* of this blueprint.

[6] See *Part B, Chapter 6: Social and Environmental Safeguards, Section 6.3.2—Benefit-Sharing and Partnerships* of this blueprint.

[7] See *Part B, Chapter 6: Social and Environmental Safeguards, Section 6.3—Key Building Block B: Indigenous Peoples and Local Communities: Rights and Partnerships* of this blueprint.

[8] See *Part B, Chapter 3: Carbon Crediting Projects, Section 3.4.2—Permanence* of this blueprint.

they can contribute to the project design—ensuring that the project area is appropriate having regard to ongoing activities (including productive uses) on the land, and that obligations to maintain the area are clearly defined, appropriately shared, and adequately resourced.

For ADB DMCs seeking to establish their own domestic crediting systems, it is important to set out defined processes for consultation, consent, and partnership among stakeholders. Doing so helps to ensure:

(i) that appropriate safeguards are in place to protect individuals and communities involved in or impacted by carbon crediting projects;
(ii) the integrity and durability of project outcomes;
(iii) clarity regarding the rights required to undertake carbon crediting projects and to sell the resulting credits; and
(iv) clear guidance for project proponents on their responsibilities toward landowners and rights holders, including how to fulfill them.

This remains an important consideration for ADB DMCs seeking to regulate projects conducted under international carbon crediting schemes. While international standards typically require project proponents to hold the legal right to carry out the project and to consult and obtain consent from key stakeholders, land tenure and stewardship issues are often highly localized. Domestic laws governing landownership and management can vary significantly between jurisdictions, sometimes resulting in confusion when applying these international rules in a domestic context, or gaps in the protection of landowners and rights holders. To address this, ADB DMCs may consider introducing *additional* legal requirements and processes—beyond those imposed by international standards—for project proponents to undertake consultation, obtain consent, and engage with landowners, rights holders, local communities, and other land stewards.

In some legal contexts, other parties—such as mortgagees—may hold a legal or beneficial interest in the land but have limited incentive or motivation to actively engage in the project. The legal framework could therefore set out the process for obtaining consent from such parties, even though their involvement in project activities may be minimal.

What this looks like in a legal framework will vary significantly depending on national circumstances, particularly the domestic legal regime governing land rights and ownership, as well as the role of Indigenous Peoples and local communities in land stewardship. At a minimum, legal frameworks should:

(i) **Require proponents to seek and maintain FPIC** from rights holders, with particular attention to the rights of Indigenous Peoples and local communities as enshrined under international law. The practical implementation of FPIC should be developed in consultation with relevant rights holders and stakeholders and must consider prevailing land tenure regimes;
(ii) **Encourage the meaningful participation of Indigenous Peoples and local communities as project owners or equal partners**—rather than solely as "stakeholders" to be consulted and whose consent is required—in carbon crediting projects undertaken on land they own, steward, or maintain an active connection to; and
(iii) **Include provisions for governance and grievance mechanisms** that safeguard the rights of Indigenous Peoples and local communities and provide avenues for addressing concerns effectively.

These concepts are discussed further in *Part B, Chapter 6: Social and Environmental Safeguards, Section 6.3—Key Building Block B: Indigenous Peoples and Local Communities: Rights and Partnerships.*

Where land laws recognize multiple forms of landownership, the legal framework could include tailored consent requirements and procedures for each landownership model (e.g., communal, government, private). ADB DMCs should also assess whether existing land tenure laws sufficiently protect rights holders and any other communities potentially impacted by a carbon crediting project, and consider reforms where gaps exist. For example, carbon crediting projects may be undertaken within the territories of Indigenous Peoples and local communities—including areas where legal recognition of historic, traditional, or customary land claims is limited or unresolved. In such contexts, robust safeguards are essential to ensure the full and equitable participation of Indigenous Peoples and local communities in carbon markets, whether the ADB DMC is pursuing a domestic crediting system or aligning with international carbon standards.

3.3 Key Building Block B: Methodologies and Crediting Standards

Carbon crediting schemes provide the framework for registering and monitoring carbon crediting projects, and for issuing carbon credits. Each scheme has a standard that defines the rules and requirements projects must satisfy to qualify for registration and credit issuance. Supporting these standards are methodologies, which detail the activities project proponents can undertake to generate verified emissions reductions or removals that can be credited under that standard. Examples of typical activities and methodologies used in carbon crediting standards are provided in Appendix 2.

The rules and requirements of the crediting standard, together with the scientific and technical specifications of its methodologies, underpin the environmental integrity of the carbon credits generated. In particular, the robustness of the calculations and assumptions used to quantify GHG removals or reductions from project activities is critical to the credibility of those credits.

Carbon crediting schemes are administered either by independent entities, governments, or, in the case of the Paris Agreement Crediting Mechanism (PACM), by the Article 6.4 "Supervisory Body" (referred to collectively in this blueprint as the "scheme administrator"). The scheme administrator is responsible for reviewing and approving the registration of projects that align with the scheme's standard and the chosen project methodology, and for issuing carbon credits once emissions reductions or removals have been verified by third parties.

Independent voluntary carbon crediting schemes have typically been administered by independent entities, including Verra (Figure 8) and Gold Standard. By contrast, some domestic voluntary markets have emerged from national carbon crediting schemes, such as the Australian Carbon Credit Unit (ACCU) scheme. However, these domestically administered schemes have often seen less uptake by buyers compared to those run by independent entities, unless strong policy incentives—such as allowing the domestic credits for compliance use—drive demand.

Figure 8: Sample Carbon Crediting Scheme Structure (Using the Verified Carbon Standard)

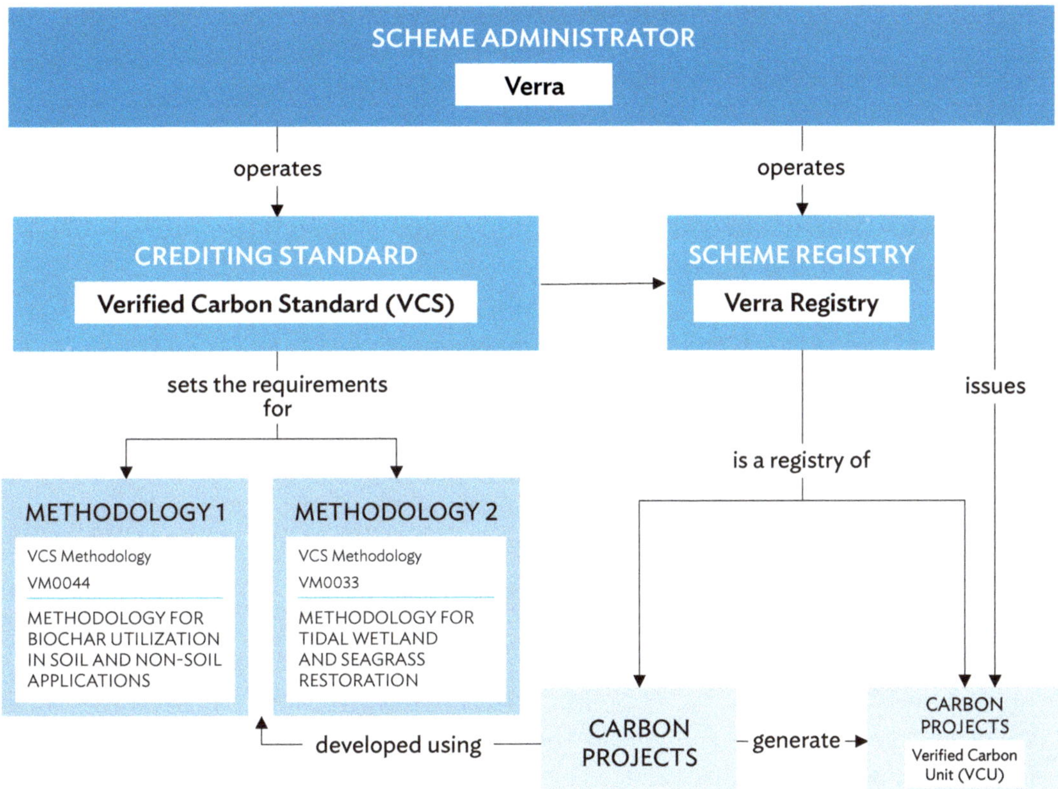

Source: Figure developed for this blueprint by the Asian Development Bank and Pollination.

3.3.1 ADB DMCs Choosing to Develop a Domestic, Government-Led Scheme

ADB DMCs may choose to establish domestic methodologies and crediting standards to exercise greater control over carbon crediting projects within their jurisdiction. However, building market confidence in the robustness of newly developed government-led methodologies and standards can take time. If the methodologies are not seen as scientifically sound or fail to credibly quantify emissions reductions or removals, they are unlikely to attract buyers and investors. Nonetheless, a domestic scheme can offer governments greater oversight over the types of projects permitted and how carbon credits are generated in their country.

When considering this approach, ADB DMCs should assess whether they have the necessary technical expertise, institutional capabilities, and financial resources to establish and operate a domestic carbon crediting scheme—including the development of methodologies—and determine where demand for the resulting credits would come from. In some cases, it may be more efficient and effective to leverage existing international crediting standards, which already have established markets and buyer confidence.

ADB DMCs seeking to develop a domestic, government-led scheme will need to:

(i) **Establish a national registry** for issuing, transferring, and canceling carbon credits;[9]

(ii) **Develop and approve project methodologies**, or adopt existing methodologies from international standards). In doing so, ADB DMCs could establish criteria for assessing methodologies, including:

  (a) alignment with relevant integrity principles, whether domestically defined or recognized under international initiatives, such as the Integrity Council for the Voluntary Carbon Market (ICVCM);

  (b) input from any independent integrity advisory body (if such a body forms part of the governance structure); and

  (c) evaluation of potential negative environmental, economic, or social impacts associated with implementing projects under the methodology;

(iii) **Assess project eligibility** based on requirements set out in the legal framework. These typically include:

  (a) jurisdictional requirements (e.g., that the project is conducted within national borders);

  (b) compliance with an approved methodology specific to the project's activity type;

  (c) adherence to integrity criteria, especially additionality;[10]

  (d) evidence of ongoing FPIC from landowners, rights holders, and other project partners and stakeholders;[11]

  (e) demonstration of compliance with social, environmental, and cultural safeguards (see Section 6.2), including securing any required permits;[12] and

  (f) alignment with national sustainable development goals and policy priorities.[13]

(iv) **Review periodic project reports**, including third-party verification and audit findings; and

(v) **Issue carbon credits** to project proponents through the national registry.

3.3.2 Adopting International Carbon Crediting Standards, Methodologies, and Registries

ADB DMCs can also choose to approve methodologies developed under international carbon crediting schemes. In doing so, they may:

(i) **Approve specific international carbon crediting standards** under which domestic carbon crediting projects can be conducted, or maintain a regularly updated list of approved methodologies. When selecting standards or methodologies to approve, ADB DMCs should

---

9 See *Part B: Chapter 4: Carbon Credits, Section 4.3—Key Building Block B: Registration of Carbon Credits* of this blueprint.

10 See *Part B, Chapter 3: Carbon Crediting Projects, Section 3.4—Key Building Block C: Approach to Managing Integrity* of this blueprint.

11 For further details, see *Part B, Chapter 3: Carbon Crediting Projects, Section 3.2.3—Consents from Third Parties with Legal Interests in Land* with respect to rights holders, and *Part B, Chapter 6: Social and Environmental Safeguards, Section 6.3—Key Building Block B: Indigenous Peoples and Local Communities: Rights and Partnerships* with respect to Indigenous Peoples and local communities, more specifically.

12 See *Part B, Chapter 6: Social and Environmental Safeguards, Section 6.2—Key Building Block A: General Safeguards* of this blueprint.

13 Additional eligibility criteria will apply if the ADB DMC intends to participate in Article 6 of the Paris Agreement. For further details, see *Part B, Chapter 5: Article 6 Requirements, Section 5.2—Key Building Block A: Authorization* of this blueprint.

consider the type of demand they intend to attract. For instance, a country aiming to supply credits to Carbon Offsetting and Reduction Scheme for International Aviation (CORSIA) buyers should approve CORSIA-eligible methodologies;

(ii) **Allow the use of third-party registries** operated by the relevant international carbon crediting scheme, and consider parallel tracking of credits generated under these schemes in a domestic informational registry, if one exists. *Part B: Chapter 4: Carbon Credits, Section 4.3—Key Building Block B: Registration of Carbon Credits* contains further details on registries.

(iii) **Establish a process for assessing and approving projects that applies additional eligibility criteria** beyond those mandated by the relevant international carbon crediting scheme. These may include, for example, that:

(a) the project uses an approved international carbon crediting standard and methodology;
(b) the project is additional and likely to generate emissions reductions or removals that are real, measurable, and verified;
(c) the project aligns with the ADB DMC's sustainable development goals;
(d) the project proponent has obtained the necessary consents from landowners, rights holders, and other stakeholders; and
(e) the project complies with specific safeguards adopted by the ADB DMC.[14]

ADB DMCs seeking to either directly participate in the PACM, or enable their activity participants to do so, must indicate to the Supervisory Body the types of Article 6.4 activities that they would consider approving for use under the mechanism.[15] This is a requirement for Article 6.4 participation.

3.3.3 Combination Approach

Finally, ADB DMCs may adopt a combination of approaches, allowing project proponents to use international crediting standards (subject to domestic regulation) alongside the issuance of domestic carbon credits based on locally developed methodologies.

Some countries take an iterative approach, initially leveraging methodologies developed for international carbon crediting schemes developing their own domestic methodologies over time.

This hybrid model can offer several benefits for ADB DMCs, including:

(i) reducing the cost, capacity burden, and time involved in developing domestic methodologies for eligible project activities; and

(ii) providing flexibility to tailor carbon credit methodologies to national circumstances—such as ecological conditions and policy priorities—and, where appropriate, align them with priority actions needed to meet nationally determined contributions (NDCs) and other national goals. Some jurisdictions may find it quicker to develop their own methodologies rather than adopting international standards.

These advantages must be carefully balanced against the additional complexity associated with having different carbon credit methodologies in operation in the ADB DMC's jurisdiction—and

[14] See *Part B, Chapter 6: Social and Environmental Safeguards* of this blueprint.
[15] UNFCC, CMA. 2021. Decision 3/CMA.3. Part IV, para. 26(e).

therefore different carbon credits being issued, traded, and retired. This could potentially lead to market segmentation and pricing discrepancies depending on the supply and perceived integrity of credits generated under domestic versus international methodologies.

Regardless of the approach taken, ADB DMCs should consider incorporating transitional provisions into their carbon crediting legal frameworks. These provisions would apply to projects being undertaken within their jurisdictions, as well as any standards and methodologies already being used by project proponents within the country. Transitional provisions should address:

(i) Whether existing projects will be required to meet any new eligibility criteria introduced by the legal framework, and the process for obtaining such approval; and

(ii) Whether existing (and new) projects may continue utilizing standards and methodologies already in use in the country, or whether they must be updated or re-approved—and the process for doing so.

INTERNATIONAL EXAMPLE

Ghana's national Article 6 framework includes specific provisions for domestic carbon markets and institutional arrangements, including the establishment of a national registry for carbon projects. It also sets out processes to recognize and track voluntary carbon market projects. While the framework initially relies on the use of pre-approved methodologies from existing international crediting standards, it also outlines Ghana's intention to gradually develop its own domestic standards and methodologies.[a]

[a] Government of Ghana. 2022. *Ghana's Framework on International Carbon Markets and Non-Market Approaches*. News release.

Source: Asian Development Bank and Pollination.

3.4 Key Building Block C: Approaches to Integrity Assurance

Over the past decade, international carbon markets have grown considerably. However, they have also faced significant scrutiny, particularly concerning the environmental integrity of the carbon and non-carbon outcomes claimed.

Regardless of whether an ADB DMC establishes a domestic carbon crediting scheme or utilizes an international one, introducing domestic laws or adopting standards that mandate minimum integrity requirements promotes the generation of high-quality carbon credits that produce positive climate, social, and ecological outcomes for both people and nature.[16] In addition, projects that meet higher integrity thresholds are more likely to command premium prices in the carbon market. Adoption of—or alignment with—existing integrity standards (including those set out in Appendix 2, Table A2.3 of this blueprint) can drive demand and position the country to attract carbon finance.

[16] Voluntary Carbon Markets Integrity Initiative (VCMI). 2023. *VCM Access Strategy Toolkit: Considerations for Host Countries When Engaging in High-Integrity Voluntary Carbon Markets*.

ADB DMCs might also find these standards useful for further guidance on regulating integrity, in addition to the options detailed below.

Integrity in a carbon crediting scheme can be managed at multiple levels:

(i) At the level of the crediting standard, which will often set the eligibility criteria for methodologies and projects;
(ii) Through methodology-specific requirements, which can significantly impact the integrity of the credits generated; and
(iii) At the individual project level, where project proponents are responsible for ensuring the integrity of their own activities.

For ADB DMCs, the way integrity is regulated—and at what level—will largely depend on whether the country is establishing its own carbon crediting scheme or authorizing the use of international schemes within its jurisdiction. International carbon crediting schemes will already have some integrity requirements embedded within their standards and methodologies. In such cases, the ADB DMC must determine what additional integrity provisions, if any, should be applied beyond those existing requirements.

The specific considerations for each approach are outlined in the sections below. Regardless of the model chosen, ADB DMCs may wish to adopt a high-level statement of integrity principles in their legal framework—for example, by incorporating such principles in the objectives and principles section of the introductory provisions.[17] Doing so helps ensure that the overarching purpose of the legal framework is grounded in a commitment to high integrity.

3.4.1 Additionality

Best practice requires that emissions reductions or removals from a mitigation activity be additional, i.e., that they "would not have occurred in the absence of the incentive created by carbon credit revenues."[18]

ADB DMCs could consider several legislative elements regarding additionality, such as requiring that:

(i) Project activities have not yet commenced, or a final investment decision in the project has not been made;
(ii) Project activities are not already mandated under existing laws or regulations; and
(iii) The project is unlikely to be funded or proceed under an alternative government initiative, support scheme, or policy-driven incentive.

To encourage the implementation of less established project types, ADB DMCs could consider specifying certain early-stage scoping activities—such as pilot activities conducted within defined parameters—that would not disqualify a project from being considered additional.

---

17 See *Part B, Chapter 1: Introductory Provisions, Section 1.2—Objectives and Principles* of this blueprint.

18 ICVCM. N.d. Core Carbon Principles.

ADB DMCs developing a domestic carbon crediting scheme should, at a minimum, require projects to demonstrate additionality as part of the project eligibility criteria. Furthermore, they should consider outlining specific approaches for demonstrating additionality, set out in regulations or guidance notes, to allow for flexible updates in line with evolving integrity standards. For example, the ICVCM *Core Carbon Principles Assessment Framework* identifies several approaches that carbon crediting standards might use to demonstrate additionality under the framework, such as investment analysis or barrier analysis (with market penetration or common practice tests), or standardized approaches.[19]

On the other hand, ADB DMCs intending to use international carbon crediting standards should also ensure that any approved standard includes a requirement for additionality. They may establish this as an approval criterion for international carbon crediting standards to be recognized under domestic regulations. In addition—or as an alternative—ADB DMCs may include a general provision in their legal framework requiring that all projects approved under the regulations demonstrate additionality. Compliance with this requirement could be shown, for example, by project proponents demonstrating how they meet the additionality criteria of the international carbon crediting standard under which the project is proposed to be registered.

INTERNATIONAL EXAMPLE

Under Zambia's Green Economy and Climate Change Act, 2024, project proponents are required to obtain authorization from the director of green economy and climate change to trade carbon credits. In deciding whether to grant this authorization, the director must have regard to:

(i) the preservation of environmental integrity;
(ii) the avoidance of double counting;
(iii) the participation of and benefit-sharing with local communities in profits from carbon trading;
(iv) the demonstration of additionality; and
(v) the promotion of sustainable development.[a]

[a] Government of Zambia. 2024. *Green Economy and Climate Change Act, 2024*. Section 24(5).

Source: Asian Development Bank and Pollination.

3.4.2 Permanence

Permanence refers to the long-lasting outcome of emissions reductions or the sustained storage of removed emissions. All mitigation activities should aim to deliver long-term and persistent mitigation benefits. Achieving this requires ensuring that the climate outcomes of a project are safeguarded and not reversed by future actions or events.

If an ADB DMC chooses to establish its own carbon crediting scheme, it should define permanence requirements within the legal framework. There are several regulatory approaches ADB DMCs can consider to address permanence:

[19] ICVCM. 2024. *Core Carbon Principles, Assessment Framework And Assessment Procedure*. p. 32.

(i) **Uniform permanence periods.** Set a fixed permanence period applicable to all projects carried out in the jurisdiction. This offers clarity to project developers and investors and supports environmental integrity.

(ii) **Differentiated permanence periods.** Establish varying permanence periods based on project type. An extended period can help ensure permanence and higher integrity projects.

(iii) **Scheme-level safeguards.** Include additional safeguards at the scheme level to mitigate the risk of non-permanence. For example, credits could be discounted by a certain percentage to account for the risk of reversal. Alternatively, the legal framework could offer project proponents the option to elect a shorter permanence period in exchange for a discounted credit volume.

(iv) **Buffer mechanisms.** Where a domestic carbon crediting standard is established, introduce a buffer reserve to address potential reversals (e.g., due to natural events). A portion of issued credits may be required to be set aside in a "pooled buffer reserve." If an emissions reversal event occurs, an equivalent number of credits are retired from this reserve to compensate for the reversal.[20]

(v) **Proponent liability for reversals.** Require project proponents to relinquish a specified number of credits if, in relation to carbon sequestration projects:

  (a) Carbon removals have been reversed;
  (b) The reversal is deemed significant; and
  (c) The reversal does not result from either:
    - a natural event beyond human control (e.g., fire, storm, pest outbreak); or
    - actions by third parties beyond the control of the project proponent.

  ADB DMCs may also require proponents to relinquish credits even in these cases if they failed to take reasonable measures to reduce or manage the impact of the natural event or the third party's actions.

(vi) **Registry-based cancellation.** Empower the registry operator to "cancel" carbon credits where a reversal has occurred.[21] However, while this approach may provide a strong integrity safeguard, it could significantly impact market participants, particularly credit purchasers. It should thus be considered carefully in light of other options listed above.[22]

If an ADB DMC chooses to use international crediting standards, incorporating the permanence period of the standard into domestic law can strengthen the DMC's enforcement powers—such as requiring credit relinquishment—by providing a legal basis for ensuring the durability of project outcomes, rather than relying solely on the rules of the international standard.

[20] J. Hacking et al. 2021. *Beyond Carbon Credits: A Blueprint for High-Quality Interventions That Work for People, Nature and Climate*. World Wildlife Fund. While the use of "buffer pools" is currently standard market practice, the treatment of reversals may ultimately be influenced by the property law principles of a given jurisdiction as the market continues to evolve.

[21] The draft UNIDROIT principles on the legal nature of verified carbon credits contain a draft principle on the cancellation of verified carbon credits upon a reversal, which may be helpful for ADB DMCs to refer to in this context. UNIDROIT. 2025. Draft UNIDROIT Principles on the Legal Nature of Verified Carbon Credits. Note that the principles are still in draft form and are subject to ongoing discussion.

[22] See *Part B, Chapter 4: Carbon Credits, Section 4.4.3—Cancellation and Retirement* of this blueprint.

INTERNATIONAL EXAMPLE

Under Australia's Carbon Credits (Carbon Farming Initiative) Act 2011, project proponents undertaking "sequestration offset projects"—those that store carbon in living biomass, dead organic matter, or soil—may choose either a 100-year or a 25-year permanence period. If the 25-year option is selected, the number of credits issued is discounted by 20%, or by another percentage specified in legislative rules at the beginning of the crediting period.

The Clean Energy Regulator may also require a project proponent to relinquish a specified number of carbon credits if a declaration of an eligible offset project is reversed, or if a carbon reversal occurs in relation to a sequestration offset project and one of the following conditions is met:

(i) The reversal is deemed significant;

(ii) The reversal is not attributable to a natural disturbance, reasonable bushfire risk reduction activities, or conduct by a third party outside the reasonable control of the proponent; or

(iii) The reversal is attributable to a natural disturbance or third-party conduct outside the proponent's reasonable control, but the proponent failed to take reasonable steps to mitigate the effect of the natural disturbance or conduct.[a]

Under Fiji's Climate Change Act 2021, if there is a material reversal or loss of carbon stocks during the permanence period of a Fijian emissions reduction project, program, or activity—whether involving forests, blue carbon, or other activity types prescribed by regulations made under the act—the project proponent must notify the climate change director as soon as practicable after becoming aware of the reversal or loss of carbon stocks. The director may, by writing, require the proponent to remedy the reversal or loss. The proponent may comply with this requirement within 90 days by either:

(i) submitting a remediation plan to the director; or

(ii) purchasing and cancelling a number of Fijian mitigation outcome units, or other emissions reduction units approved by the director, equivalent to the reversal or loss of carbon stocks.

If the proponent fails to implement the remediation plan to the director's satisfaction, or does not purchase and retire the equivalent number of Fijian mitigation outcome units, the director may revoke the approval for the project to operate in Fiji.

The minister for climate change also has the power to make regulations defining the circumstances under which a protection order or other arrangement may be imposed in relation to an area of forest, blue carbon, or other project, program, or activity type (as prescribed by regulations) that has been subject to a reversal or loss of carbon stocks.[b]

[a] Government of Australia. 2024. *Carbon Credits (Carbon Farming Initiative) Act 2011*, as amended as of 14 October 2024. Sections 16, 27(3)(f), 54, 86A, 87, 89, 90, and 91.

[b] Government of Fiji. 2021. *Climate Change Act 2021*. Section 54.

Source: Asian Development Bank and Pollination.

3.4.3 No Double Counting

Double counting occurs when a single emissions reduction or removal is counted by more than one entity toward achieving international mitigation compliance targets or goals in the context of the Paris Agreement (e.g., in country-to-country or CORSIA transfers).

The risk of double counting of carbon credits can in part be mitigated through technical design features in national registries, supported by legislative measures, including:

(i) Rules governing the operation of the registry, including a requirement that each carbon credit be assigned a unique serial number to ensure traceability and prevent duplication;
(ii) Explicit provisions addressing double counting, such as a prohibition on issuing credits for emissions reductions or removals that have already been used to generate other credits; and
(iii) Integration of the carbon market framework with Article 6 processes and procedures, including mechanisms for the authorization of credits and application of corresponding adjustments.[23]

Countries may also consider introducing specific regulations or guidance to address double claiming and double use, which should align with applicable consumer protection laws.

Double claiming occurs when the same emissions reduction or removal "is claimed by two different entities toward achieving mitigation targets or goals."[24] A common example is when a company purchases carbon credits from a project in a host country to offset its emissions, while the host country also includes the reductions from that same project toward its nationally determined contribution (NDC) under the Paris Agreement.

Double use, by contrast, arises "when the same carbon offset is counted twice toward achieving mitigation targets or goals,"[25] such as when the same carbon credit is used or retired more than once—either by the same entity or by different entities—to claim an emissions reduction or offset.

These risks are relevant for ADB DMCs establishing domestic crediting schemes and those authorizing the use of international carbon crediting standards. Addressing them through clear legal and regulatory provisions is essential to maintain environmental integrity and market credibility.

3.4.4 Real, Measurable, and Verifiable

Carbon credits must be based on a realistic and credible baseline, along with quantified, monitored, reported, and independently verified assumptions, in order to ensure environmental integrity. This is often managed through several processes within a carbon crediting scheme:

(i) **At the standard level**, through eligibility requirements for projects and carbon credits, and obligations for project proponents to monitor outcomes and obtain independent verification of these outcomes before credits are issued; and
(ii) **Through approved methodologies**, which set out requirements and procedures for determining project boundaries, establishing baselines, monitoring key parameters, and ultimately quantifying GHG emissions reductions or removals generated from the project. These requirements are usually based on technical assessments tailored to relevant mitigation activity types and are essential to ensuring that emissions reductions and removals are real, accurate, and conservatively ascertained.

---

23 See *Part B, Chapter 5: Article 6 Requirements* of this blueprint.
24 World Wildlife Fund, et al. 2020. What Makes a High-Quality Carbon Credit? p. 3.
25 Footnote 24, p. 4.

ADB DMCs may consider different legislative elements to ensure that credited emissions reductions or removals are real, measurable, and verifiable, depending on whether they are establishing a domestic carbon crediting scheme or using international crediting standards.

Where an ADB DMC opts to recognize international crediting standards, it could introduce requirements such as:

(i) **Project-level assurance.** All project proponents must ensure that emissions reductions or removals credited from projects carried out domestically are real, measurable, and capable of being independently verified.

(ii) **Standard-level assessment.** The decision-making authority responsible for approving the use of international crediting standards and methodologies must consider whether the emissions reductions or removals to be credited or recognized under the carbon market framework meet the threshold of being real, measurable, and verifiable.

If ADB DMCs are establishing their own domestic carbon crediting scheme, they could:

(i) **Define emissions reductions or removals accordingly.** Incorporate "real, measurable, and capable of being verified" into the definition of an emissions reduction or removal;

(ii) **Set methodology eligibility criteria.** Ensure that the eligibility criteria for approving methodologies under the scheme require the decision maker to assess whether the methodology is likely to generate emissions reductions or removals that are real, measurable, and conservatively quantified; and

(iii) **Include robust MRV obligations.** Require project proponents to monitor, report, and obtain independent verification of emissions reductions or removals resulting from mitigation activities carried out in the country. These obligations should align with the monitoring, reporting, and verification (MRV) provisions discussed in *Part B, Chapter 7: Monitoring and Enforcement* of this blueprint.

3.4.5 Leakage

Leakage refers to the net increase in GHG emissions or decrease in removals that occurs outside a project's boundaries but is attributable to the project's mitigation activities. "These include, for example, indirect emission changes upstream or downstream of the mitigation activity or rebound effects."[26] To maintain environmental integrity, potential increases in emissions outside the project boundary should be assessed and mitigated.

Carbon market procedures and architecture incorporate several mechanisms to manage leakage risks. The assessment process for approving carbon crediting methodologies typically considers whether and how the methodology addresses leakage—specifically, whether it identifies key sources of leakage, includes mitigation measures, and accounts for material sources of leakage in the quantification of emissions reductions or removals.[27]

---

[26] World Wildlife Fund (WWF-US) et al. 2022. Methodology for Assessing the Quality of Carbon Credits. p. 5.

[27] Criterion 10.5, *Quantification of Emissions or Removals from the Mitigation Activity*, in the Integrity Council for the Voluntary Carbon Market's (ICVCM) *Core Carbon Principles Assessment Framework and Procedure*, may offer useful guidance for ADB DMCs. This criterion sets out parameters to ensure that emissions reductions or removals are quantified in a manner that enables "conservativeness and robust quantification." ICVCM. 2024. Assessment Framework (Version 1.1).

Some methodologies and standards require leakage to be "estimated and monitored using an approved approach," with any identified leakage subtracted from the quantification of carbon credits issued.[28] Some Verified Carbon Standard (VCS) methods, for instance, require leakage to be assessed for 5 years following the start of a project.[29] The rationale is that this time frame captures the period during which "the effects of leakage from displaced agricultural production are expected to occur." The VCS further notes that "effects arising more than 5 years after the commencement of a project activity are unlikely to meet the standards for being reasonably attributable to the project activity."

Specific approaches to mitigating leakage may be adopted for particular methodology types. In the case of REDD+ projects, leakage is addressed through jurisdictional REDD+ programs, which monitor deforestation across an entire jurisdiction. This broader monitoring allows for the identification and management of deforestation that may be displaced from the project area to other locations within the jurisdiction.

Whether ADB DMCs choose to recognize international carbon crediting standards for use in their jurisdiction, establish their own domestic crediting scheme, or adopt a hybrid approach, it is essential that they are confident that leakage is appropriately addressed. To support this, ADB DMCs could consider incorporating the following measures:

(i) **Inclusion of specific provisions on leakage** within carbon market legislation and/or regulatory frameworks—for example, a general requirement that any mitigation activity registered or approved under the framework must not result in increased emissions elsewhere;

(ii) **Requirements for methodologies to consider and account** for material sources of leakage within their GHG emissions calculation methods, as a condition of approval under the domestic carbon market framework; and

(iii) **Assessment of international carbon crediting standards and methodologies** approved for use in the jurisdiction to ensure that they include robust procedures to assess and account for material sources of leakage in their GHG emissions calculation methods.

28 Plan Vivo. N.d. Leakage.

29 Verified Carbon Standard. 2023. VMD0054 Module for Estimating Leakage from ARR Activities; Verified Carbon Standard. 2012. Estimation of Emissions from Activity-Shifting Leakage.

A traditional outrigger boat along a tropical shoreline in Palawan, Philippines. Coastal communities can support community-based conservation and ecotourism-linked carbon crediting projects that promote sustainable livelihoods and environmental stewardship (photo by Ariel Javellana/ADB).

CHAPTER 4

CARBON CREDITS

Carbon credits translate emissions reductions and removals into a transferable unit recorded in a registry. These credits can be transferred between owners, both domestically and internationally, through the registry infrastructure.

If an ADB DMC chooses to establish its own carbon crediting scheme, it must implement legislative provisions governing the issuance, registration, and transfer of carbon credits. Where an ADB DMC draws on existing international schemes, it can leverage the schemes' carbon credit issuance processes and registries. Figure 9 outlines the recommended building blocks for provisions concerning the issuance, registration, and transfer of carbon credits:

Figure 9: Carbon Credits—Building Blocks and Constituent Elements

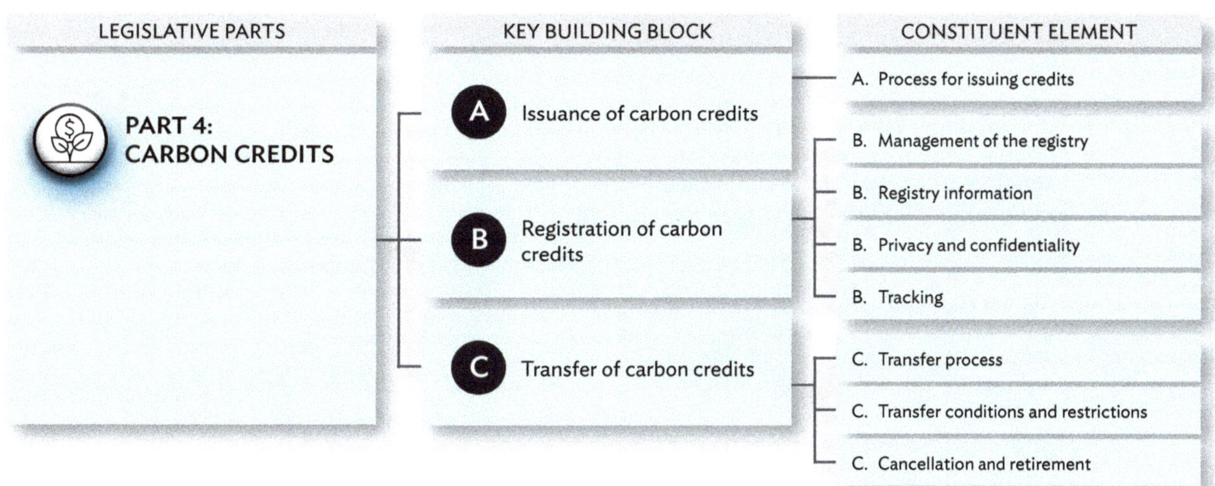

Source: Figure developed for this blueprint by the Asian Development Bank and Pollination.

4.1 Summary of Fundamental Building Blocks Likely to Be Required

Table 6 summarizes the fundamental building blocks likely to be required for provisions on the issuance, registration, and transfer of carbon credits in ADB DMCs, with building blocks related to domestic carbon crediting schemes shown on the left, and those related to international carbon crediting standards on the right.

**Table 6: Issuance, Registration, and Transfer of Carbon Credits—
Fundamental Building Blocks Likely to Be Required**

FUNDAMENTAL BUILDING BLOCKS LIKELY TO BE REQUIRED	
ADB DMC Establishing a Domestic Carbon Crediting Scheme	**ADB DMC Utilizing International Carbon Crediting Standards**
✓ Process for issuing carbon credits, including: - Power to issue carbon credits; - Requirements for project proponents to report and obtain independent verification of emissions reductions or removals achieved within a defined time frame; and - Clear procedures governing the issuance process.	✕ A carbon credits issuance process is not required, as this function is handled by the scheme administrator.
✓ Registration of carbon credits through the establishment of a scheme registry, including: - Responsibility for maintaining and managing the registry; - Registry information, including the recording and tracking of carbon crediting projects and the credits they generate under the domestic scheme, as well as any projects and credits developed under international carbon crediting schemes (if permitted for use in the ADB DMC); - Provisions addressing privacy and confidentiality; and - Tracking mechanisms to ensure carbon credits and their status can be accurately recorded and monitored within the registry.	? While not mandatory, it is advisable for ADB DMCs to establish at least a basic informational registry to track carbon crediting projects undertaken within the country and the credits they generate. Doing so will provide greater visibility into domestic carbon crediting activities. ✓ ADB DMCs intending to participate in Article 6 of the Paris Agreement will also require a system to track mitigation outcomes generated by carbon crediting projects in their jurisdiction that are authorized for international transfer (see *Part B, Chapter 5: Article 6 Requirements* of this blueprint).
✓ Transfer of carbon credits, including: - Process for carbon credit holders to apply for, and for the scheme administrator to effect, transfers of carbon credits within the scheme registry and to external registries; - Consideration of any necessary amendments or additions to domestic laws that may affect the transfer of carbon credits, such as laws governing the sale and transfer of property and interests in property, financial products and exchanges, and taxation; and - Transfer restrictions and conditions, particularly relevant for ADB DMCs seeking to engage in Article 6 of the Paris Agreement (see *Part B, Chapter 5: Article 6 Requirements* of this blueprint).	✓ Transfer of carbon credits, including: - Consideration of any necessary amendments or additions to domestic laws that may affect the transfer of carbon credits, such as laws governing the sale and transfer of property and interests in property, financial products and exchanges, and taxation; and - Transfer restrictions and conditions, particularly relevant for ADB DMCs seeking to engage in Article 6 of the Paris Agreement (see *Part B, Chapter 5: Article 6 Requirements* of this blueprint).
✓ Cancellation of carbon credits, including provisions to facilitate the retirement of carbon credits within the scheme registry.	✕ A process for the cancellation and retirement of carbon credits is not required, as this function is carried out by the scheme administrator.

ADB = Asian Development Bank, DMC = developing member country.

Legend: ✓ likely to be required.
? not likely to be required but with details for determination.
✕ not likely to be required.

Source: ADB and Pollination.

4.2 Key Building Block A: Issuance of Carbon Credits

Carbon credits should be issued exclusively for emissions reductions or removals reported by project proponents using an approved methodology and subsequently verified by an independent verification body. In the usual procedure for carbon credit issuance, the project proponent submits a report detailing the emissions reductions and removals achieved within the specified reporting period. This report undergoes verification by an independent third-party verifier.[1] Following this, the scheme administrator thoroughly reviews the verified report. If the administrator is satisfied that the project and the reported emissions reductions and removals comply with the established scheme standards and methodology, the credits are then issued into the project proponent's registry account.

If an ADB DMC chooses to establish its own domestic voluntary crediting system, it will also need to legislate the powers and processes required for the issuance of carbon credits.

On the other hand, for ADB DMCs seeking to utilize international standards, the process for issuing carbon credits is typically governed by the rules of the relevant international carbon crediting standard and its associated registry. These DMCs should nonetheless review and understand the credit issuance processes of the selected schemes, including any specific requirements related to the timing of verification. In such cases, ADB DMCs may also wish to track the credits issued to projects within their jurisdiction—for example, to support participation in Article 6 of the Paris Agreement. This is discussed further in *Part B, Chapter 5: Article 6 Requirements, Section 5.4—Key Building Block C: Tracking* of this blueprint.

4.2.1 Process for Issuing Credits

ADB DMCs looking to establish their own domestic carbon crediting standard could consider including the following process to issue carbon credits:

(i) **Reporting and application.** Project proponents could be required to report on emissions reductions or removals achieved within a defined time period (reporting period), using an approved methodology, and submit an application for credit issuance based on this report. ADB DMCs may choose to prescribe reporting periods for different project types or allow project proponents to select them within specified parameters (e.g., minimum and maximum durations).

(ii) **Verification.** To support the integrity of the emissions reductions or removals claimed, ADB DMCs should consider requiring that reported outcomes be independently verified prior to credit issuance. This is discussed further in *Part B, Chapter 7: Monitoring and Enforcement, Section 7.2—Key Building Block A: Monitoring, Reporting, and Verification* of this blueprint.

(iii) **Certification.** Once both the project report and the independent verification report have been received and reviewed, the scheme administrator may issue formal documentation—such as a certificate—confirming the number and type of carbon credits the project proponent is entitled to for the reporting period.

(iv) **Issuance.** Provided that all relevant conditions are satisfied and the project complies with the applicable legislative and methodological requirements, the scheme administrator would then

[1] See *Part B, Chapter 7: Monitoring and Enforcement, Section 7.2—Key Building Block A: Monitoring, Reporting, and Verification* of this blueprint.

issue the specified number of credits specified in the certificate of entitlement by recording them in the appropriate registry account.

To give investors greater certainty, ADB DMCs may consider specifying clear time periods within which these actions must occur. The length of these periods can vary across jurisdictions. For instance, in Australia, the prescribed period is 90 days.[2] In Indonesia, it is 14 days.[3] Under Fiji's Climate Change Act 2021, the period for issuance of Fijian mitigation outcome units by the director of climate change is 30 days from the date the application was made.[4]

The varying periods highlight that the specific duration is less important than ensuring that clear, reasonable timelines are embedded in the legal framework. These time frames should be realistic, taking into account the DMC's institutional capacity and resource constraints. Establishing such

INTERNATIONAL EXAMPLE

Under Indonesia's Regulation of the Minister of Environment and Forestry No. 21 of 2022 on the procedures for implementing carbon pricing, project proponents must register their projects in the National Registry System for Climate Change (*Sistem Registri Nasional Perubahan Iklim* or SRN PPI). Registration requires an approved methodology and independent validation through a systematic and documented process, to ensure that the project design and activities meet the specified requirements.[a]

Following implementation of the project activities, the reported carbon sequestration and/or emissions reductions must be verified by an independent third party. This verification process involves confirming: (i) adherence to the eligibility criteria set out in the chosen methodology, (ii) the accuracy and credibility of data used in monitoring the project activities, (iii) the absence of double registration of the carbon crediting project in other certification mechanisms, and (iv) consistency in the implementation and monitoring of the project activities. Verification must be completed within 6 months of the monitoring report being submitted to the verifier.[b]

Subsequently, the project proponent must apply to the director general for the issuance of the certificate of greenhouse gas emissions reduction (*Sertifikat Pengurangan Emisi Gas Rumah Kaca* or SPE-GRK). The application must include project data; reports on monitoring, evaluation, and activity implementation; the validation and verification reports; and the requested SPE-GRK amount. The director general, in coordination with the relevant ministers, will review the application through the "MRV Team," a measurement, reporting, and verification team established by the director general. If the MRV Team determines that the application meets the necessary criteria (i.e., the results are declared "appropriate"), the director general issues the SPE-GRK within 14 days. A tariff, categorized by the regulation as non-tax state revenue, will be levied for the SPE-GRK issuance.[c]

[a] Government of Indonesia. 2022. *Regulation of the Minister of Environment and Forestry No. 21 of 2022: Procedure for Implementation of Carbon Pricing (MOEF 21/2022)*. Article 15.

[b] Footnote a, Articles 39 and 41.

[c] Footnote a, Article 66.

Source: Asian Development Bank and Pollination.

[2] Government of Australia. 2011. *Carbon Credits (Carbon Farming Initiative) Act 2011*. Section 15.

[3] Government of Indonesia. 2022. *Regulation of the Minister of Environment and Forestry No. 21 of 2022: Procedure for Implementation of Carbon Pricing*. Article 66.

[4] Government of Fiji. 2021. *Climate Change Act 2021*. Section 51(4).

time frames helps build confidence among market participants and facilitates more efficient project planning and implementation.

ADB DMCs will also need to determine how carbon credits issued under their domestic carbon crediting scheme will be identified. For example, in Australia, they are designated as Australian Carbon Credit Units (ACCUs), while in New Zealand, they are called New Zealand Units (NZUs).

ADB DMCs must likewise maintain their own registry capable of issuing these credits and effecting transfers between account holders. Further discussion of registry-related matters is provided in *Part B, Chapter 4: Carbon Credits, Section 4.3—Key Building Block B: Registration of Carbon Credits* of this blueprint.

In addition, ADB DMCs may wish to include provisions granting the authority to revoke issued credits in specific circumstances, such as to correct errors in issuance (e.g., over-crediting).

4.3 Key Building Block B: Registration of Carbon Credits

Registries serve as crucial infrastructure in carbon markets. They provide transparency, establish a legal chain of custody for the issuance and transfer of carbon credits, and make key information about carbon crediting projects publicly accessible. In addition, registries facilitate the accounting of carbon credits and can assist countries in reporting on mitigation outcomes.

Registries can be categorized into two types: (i) transactional registries, and (ii) informational (or database) registries. The key elements of each registry type are outlined in Figure 10.

Transactional registries are essential for operationalizing a carbon crediting scheme. They provide the infrastructure for the issuance, transfer, and retirement or cancellation of credits under the scheme. Most carbon crediting schemes—including independent crediting standards—maintain their own transactional registry to support these functions. For example, the Paris Agreement Crediting Mechanism (PACM) is the mechanism registry under Article 6 of the Paris Agreement.

In contrast, informational registries (also referred to as database registries) lack the transactional functionality. Instead, they simply enable countries to track carbon crediting projects and credits issued within a country, often across multiple carbon crediting schemes.

ADB DMCs have a range of options when designing registry systems to track carbon crediting projects within their jurisdiction. Table 7 outlines these options, along with key considerations.

ADB DMCs may also choose to link registries to enable the flow of information and the transaction of credits between different registries, if desired.

The key considerations for ADB DMCs when legislating on the registration of carbon credits are outlined below, to the extent that an ADB DMC opts to establish a domestic registry, i.e., Options 1 or 2 in Table 7. Additional considerations will apply for ADB DMCs intending to participate in Article 6 of the Paris Agreement, as set out in *Part B, Chapter 5: Article 6 Requirements* of this blueprint.

Figure 10: Key Elements of the Registry Process

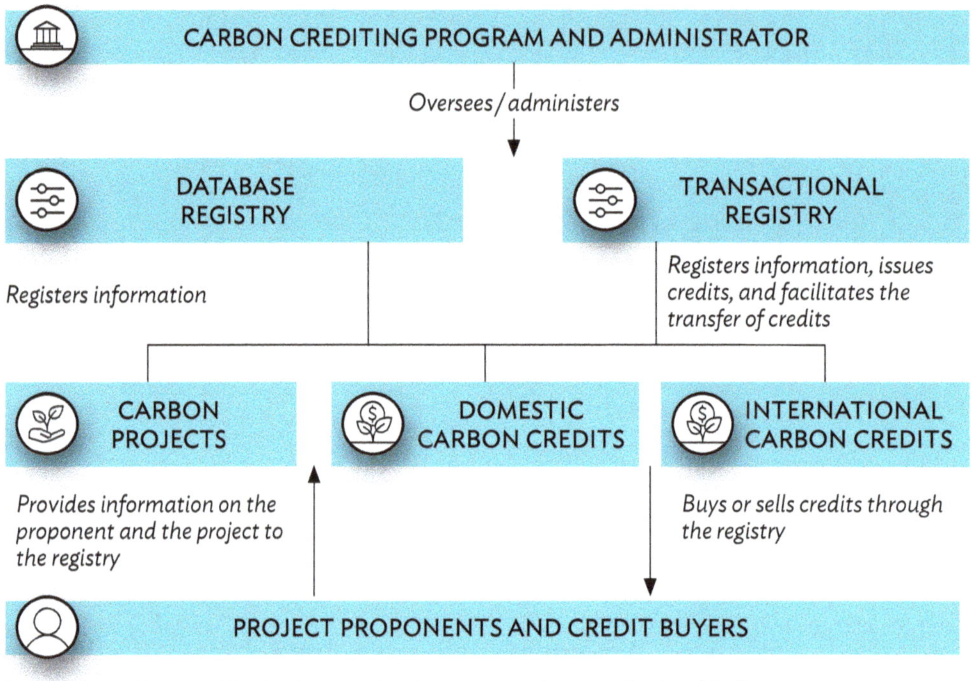

Source: Figure developed for this blueprint by the Asian Development Bank and Pollination.

Table 7: Registry Design Options

OPTION	DESCRIPTION OF KEY FEATURES	RELEVANT CONSIDERATIONS
1. Establish a domestic transactional registry	Under this option, the ADB DMC would establish its own transactional registry, which would allow for the creation of digital accounts to hold carbon credits and facilitate their transfer, cancellation, and retirement.	• This option is most appropriate for ADB DMCs that intend to establish their own domestic carbon crediting scheme, as it provides the infrastructure necessary to issue domestic credits for projects that have achieved verified mitigation outcomes. • This option requires a significant investment of domestic resources and technical capacity. To ensure integrity, the registry must operate on a secure and reliable system—typically electronic—that can maintain the accuracy of registry data and safeguard the transactions it facilitates. • The ADB DMC would also need sufficient resources and capacity to manage and maintain the registry, including processing and responding to requests from market participants in a timely and effective manner.

continued on next page

Table 7 *continued*

OPTION	DESCRIPTION OF KEY FEATURES	RELEVANT CONSIDERATIONS
2. Establish a domestic informational registry	Under this option, the ADB DMC would establish a national registry to record (i) carbon crediting projects implemented within the country under either domestic or international carbon crediting schemes, and (ii) the carbon credits issued in relation to those projects.	• This option provides the ADB DMC with a centralized overview of carbon crediting projects implemented within its jurisdiction, as well as the volume of carbon credits issued in relation to those projects. This information can be helpful for ADB DMCs as they prepare their next NDCs and implementation plans, as it offers insights into the flow of carbon finance into the country and the sectors, areas, or activities it supports. • Compared to Option 1, this approach requires fewer administrative and technical resources. Since the registry does not serve as the primary platform for issuing or transacting carbon credits, it does not need to support the creation or management of holding accounts. Consequently, the operational and maintenance demands of the registry are reduced. • This option does, however, require the ADB DMC to rely on information provided by project proponents. The ADB DMC may also supplement or verify this information using data from international carbon crediting scheme registries on projects implemented within its jurisdiction.
3. Rely upon a registry operated by the UNFCCC for purposes of Article 6	The UNFCCC will establish a registry to track ITMOs for parties to the Paris Agreement that are participating in Article 6 but lack their own national registry or access to one. While the primary function of this UNFCCC registry will be informational, the secretariat will also offer supplemental registry services upon request. These services will include the issuance of mitigation outcomes that are authorized—or intended to be authorized—by the party for international transfer. This support is designed to facilitate participation in Article 6 cooperative approaches. The supplemental services will be interoperable with the international registry established by the UNFCCC mentioned above. Importantly, while the registry may issue mitigation outcomes, this function does not constitute an endorsement by the UNFCCC of the quality of the credits.[a]	• This registry is relevant only for ADB DMCs that intend to participate Article 6 of the Paris Agreement. • By using this registry, an ADB DMC avoids the need to establish and maintain a domestic registry or to obtain access to a registry operated by an international crediting scheme. Furthermore, the registry will be aligned with UNFCCC tracking and reporting requirements and guidance for Article 6 participating countries. • A limitation of this approach is that the ADB DMC will have minimal control over the registry's functionality, which may not be tailored to its specific needs. • Moreover, the registry will only capture carbon credits that are authorized for international transfer under Article 6 rules and guidance. This means that projects conducted within the ADB DMC's jurisdiction that generate credits solely for domestic use will not be recorded. Where this is the case, the ADB DMC may lack visibility over these projects or the number of credits they generate domestically.

continued on next page

Table 7 *continued*

OPTION	DESCRIPTION OF KEY FEATURES	RELEVANT CONSIDERATIONS
4. Rely upon registries operated by international crediting schemes	Under this option, the ADB DMC would rely on information contained in the registries maintained by international carbon crediting schemes. These registries are operated by the respective scheme administrators and reflect only the projects registered and credits issued under that specific scheme.	• This option is likely most relevant for ADBDMCs that do not have the capacity or resources to establish a national registry and are not participating in Article 6 of the Paris Agreement. • A significant advantage of this approach is the availability of existing registry infrastructure, removing the need for the ADB DMC to develop or manage a domestic system. These registries also provide real-time, publicly accessible information for market stakeholders. • However, compared to Options 1 or 2, the ADB DMC may have reduced visibility over all carbon crediting projects conducted within its jurisdiction, as it would need to rely on monitoring multiple international scheme registries to track registrations, issuances, and transactions. This could also make it more difficult to enforce domestic restrictions on certain project or activity types.

ADB = Asian Development Bank, DMC = developing member country, ITMO = internationally transferred mitigation outcome, NDC = nationally determined contribution, UNFCCC = United Nations Framework Convention on Climate Change.

[a] UNFCCC, Conference of the Parties Serving as the Meeting of the Parties to the Paris Agreement (CMA). 2024. Decision 4/CMA.6. Part IX, paras. 50–53.

Source: ADB and Pollination.

4.3.1 Management of the Registry

ADB DMCs should identify the entity responsible for maintaining the carbon registry. Typically, this responsibility falls on the body overseeing carbon markets in the country, which could be a newly established or existing independent government body.

This approach is especially pertinent for ADB DMCs seeking to establish a transactional registry. For example, in Australia, the Clean Energy Regulator—the governing body that manages the ACCU scheme—is responsible for managing and maintaining the Australian National Registry of Emissions Units (ANREU). As a transactional registry, ANREU enables the issuance of credits, and the Clean Energy Regulator is responsible for carrying out registry functions, such as credit issuance and processing transfers between registry accounts at the request of account holders.

ADB DMCs may also assign responsibility for the registry to an existing government department. This approach is more likely to suit DMCs opting for Option 2 in Table 7, as the administrative and technical requirements of an informational registry are less demanding than those of a transactional registry. Moreover, informational registries are intended, in part, to inform government policy and decision-making on carbon markets—functions typically led by the relevant ministry or department. For this reason, assigning registry management to that same body may be a practical and efficient option.

4.3.2 Registry Information

Defining the information required to be recorded in the carbon credit registry can support ADB DMCs in maintaining adequate records to track projects and the credits they generate, and in meeting domestic and Paris Agreement-related carbon accounting and reporting obligations. Accordingly, ADB DMCs should take these reporting and accounting requirements into account when drafting provisions specifying the information to be included in the registry. In doing so, ADB DMCs should seek to balance administrative efficiency with the need to ensure that sufficient information is captured to:

(i) enforce the legal framework against the project proponent (e.g., understanding who the project proponent is, or where they are based);

(ii) ensure appropriate oversight over projects; and

(iii) enable reporting on mitigation outcomes and progress toward national targets (including the nationally determined contribution [NDC]) across all projects, as well as any reversals.

ADB DMCs could require the following categories of information to be recorded in the domestic registry:

(i) **Personal information**, such as:
  (a) the name of each person holding a registry account;
  (b) the address of each account holder; and
  (c) the total number of carbon credits held by each account holder.

(ii) **Project information**, such as:
  (a) the parties involved;
  (b) the project objectives;
  (c) the project's location;
  (d) the methodology used;
  (e) the sources of emissions removals or reductions;
  (f) preliminary project costs;
  (g) financing mechanisms;
  (h) estimated greengouse gas (GHG) emissions removals or reductions;
  (i) associated co-benefits; and
  (j) intended REDD+ activities (for REDD+ projects or programs).

(iii) **Crediting information**, such as:
  (a) the identifier of the originating registry (if the credit being tracked has been issued in a different registry);
  (b) the serial number of the mitigation outcome;
  (c) the date of issuance;
  (d) the vintage of the underlying mitigation outcome; and
  (e) details of any transfer, retirement, or cancellation, as applicable.

If the ADB DMC participates in Article 6, additional information may need to be recorded in the registry to align with tracking requirements under the Article 6 rules and guidance. *Part B, Chapter 5: Article 6 Requirements* of this blueprint discusses this further.

To enhance transparency, ADB DMCs could require certain information to be made publicly available through a registry, with due consideration for applicable privacy and confidentiality requirements.[5] To further support transparency and help identify trends in the domestic carbon market, ADB DMCs could also consider publishing key registry data on an annual basis. For example, at the end of each financial year, the registry could be required to disclose the total number of carbon credits issued during that period.

Furthermore, depending on how carbon credits are legally characterized under the laws of the ADB DMC, it may be possible to take security over carbon credits.[6] ADB DMCs establishing a domestic carbon crediting scheme and transactional registry could consider clarifying—whether through registry rules or other legal instruments—how security interests in carbon credits can be recognized and enforced. This could include allowing third parties holding security interests to be appointed as agents or authorized representatives for accounts in which the relevant carbon credits are held.

INTERNATIONAL EXAMPLE

The New Zealand Emission Trading Register (the registry established under the New Zealand Emissions Trading Scheme) includes functionality to recognize and enforce security interests. Within the registry, an account holder may authorize a third party to register a security interest over New Zealand Units (NZUs) held in their account. To do so, the security holder must first register as a user in the system and provide the account holder with a unique code, which enables the security interest to be linked to the relevant account. Once registered, the security interest triggers a block on the affected NZUs, preventing their transfer without the consent of the security holder.

This functionality is supported by New Zealand's Personal Property Securities Act 1999, which governs security interests over personal property.[a] Similar functionality is also being contemplated under the Article 6.4 mechanism registry, such as through the establishment of a pledge system to recognize and enforce security interests.[b]

[a] Government of New Zealand, *Te Mana Rauhī Taiao* (Environment Protection Authority). N.d. Third party security interests.

[b] UNFCCC, Article 6.4 Supervisory Body. 2025. *Information note: Legal, technical and financial implications of providing functionality for the treatment of financial security interests in Article 6.4 emissions reductions within the mechanism registry (v.01.0) (SBM015)*.

Source: Asian Development Bank and Pollination.

ADB DMCs should also consider including transitional provisions in any newly adopted legal framework to ensure that credits issued to pre-existing carbon crediting projects (i.e., those in operation prior to the adoption of the framework) can be recorded in the registry.

4.3.3 Privacy and Confidentiality

Registries may contain sensitive information, including personal details such as names, addresses, and contact information, as well as commercially sensitive project documentation. As such, privacy and confidentiality requirements are important considerations for ADB DMCs. When drafting registry-related regulations, ADB DMCs should balance the need for market transparency with privacy protections, taking into account any applicable domestic privacy and confidentiality laws.

[5] See *Part B, Chapter 4: Carbon Credits, Section 4.3.3—Privacy and Confidentiality* of this blueprint.

[6] See *Part B, Chapter 1: Introductory Provisions, Section 1.3.2—Carbon Credit* of this blueprint.

To enhance data protection, ADB DMCs could consider incorporating the following provisions into laws governing the domestic registry:

(i) A general provision that data held in the registry is subject to national data security requirements, and

(ii) A more prescriptive approach stipulating that certain categories of information—such as personal data and commercially protected information—remain confidential.

4.3.4 Tracking

Transactional and informational registries play a central role in mitigating the risk of double counting by enabling carbon crediting scheme administrators and national authorities to track and trace both projects and the carbon credits generated from them. An accurate tracking and tracing functionality is also essential for countries to participate in and comply with requirements under Article 6 of the Paris Agreement.

To support effective tracking of projects and carbon credits, ADB DMCs should consider including the following elements in their legal frameworks:

(i) Requiring each carbon credit registered in the system to have a unique serial number;

(ii) Implementing a labeling system for registered projects and credits to indicate their Article 6 authorization status.[7] Labels could also indicate the credit's status—such as "active," "canceled," or "retired"—to ensure that only "active" credits are available for retirement or cancellation; and

(iii) Requiring that units that have been "used" (i.e., retired) be transferred to a "cancellation account" in the registry, which should record the amount of credits used, their intended use, and the party or parties using the credits (particularly where the user is not the original owner of the operational account).

Additional considerations will apply if an ADB DMC is considering engaging in Article 6 cooperative approaches (see *Part B, Chapter 5: Article 6 Requirements* of this blueprint).

INTERNATIONAL EXAMPLE

Ghana's carbon market framework allows voluntary carbon market projects conducted under recognized international crediting schemes to be undertaken within the country, provided they are also registered on Ghana's national carbon registry.[a]

To ensure oversight, Ghana requires that when carbon credits are issued through the registry of a recognized international crediting scheme, the relevant international registry must transmit the issuance details for each authorized carbon credit to Ghana's Carbon Market Office within 7 days of issuance. This requirement enables Ghana to maintain visibility over credits generated under such projects.

[a] Government of Ghana. December 2022. *Ghana's Framework on International Carbon Markets and Non-Market Approaches*.
Source: Asian Development Bank and Pollination.

[7] See *Part B, Chapter 5: Article 6 Requirements* of this blueprint.

4.4 Key Building Block C: Transfer of Carbon Credits

The ability to transfer legal ownership of carbon credits is essential to the proper functioning of carbon markets. Buyers need to receive full and unencumbered legal ownership of carbon credits in their registry account to use them for compliance or voluntary purposes.[8]

Carbon credits may be sold directly to purchasers by project developers on the primary market, or subsequently traded on the secondary market through third parties, such as intermediaries or carbon exchanges. Typically, the transfer of legal title occurs within carbon credit registries, with exchanges increasingly integrating with these registries to enable faster settlement of transactions (Figure 11).

Figure 11: Carbon Credit Transfer Process in Primary and Secondary Markets

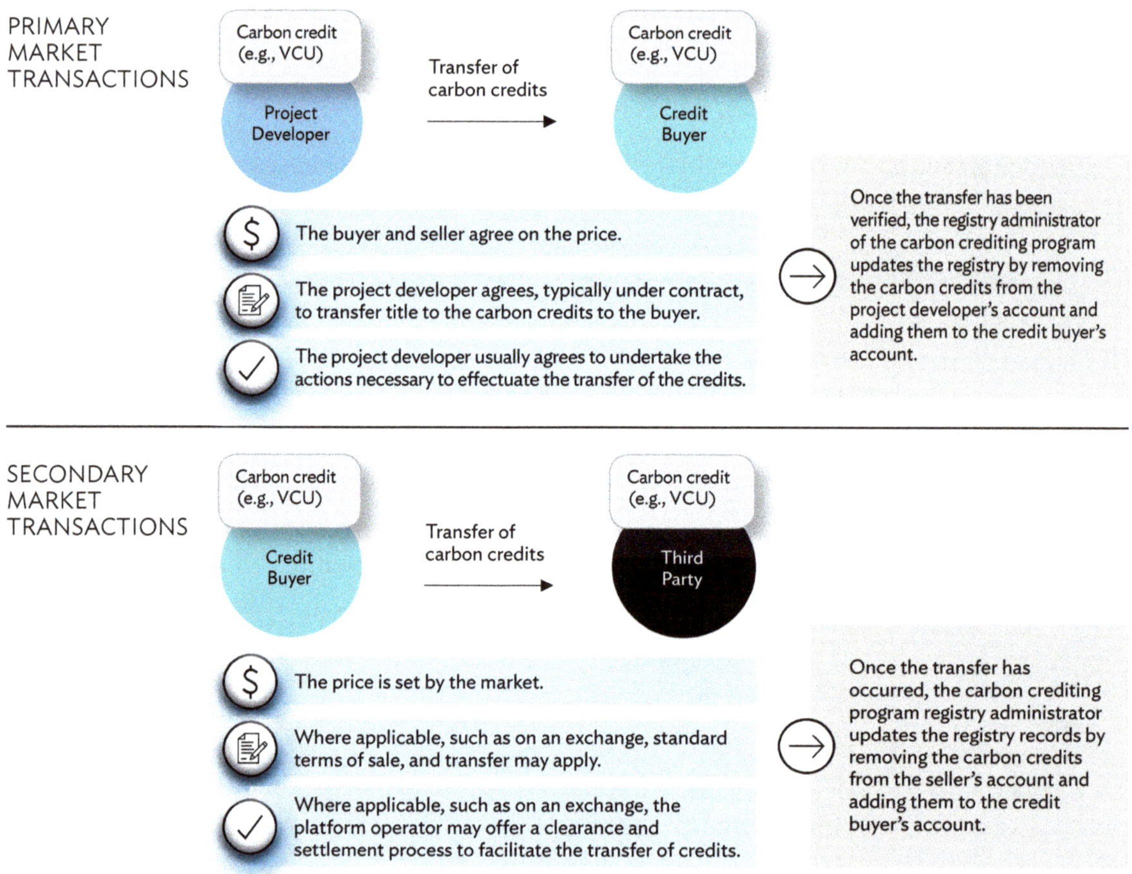

VCU = Verified Carbon Units.
Source: Figure developed for this blueprint by the Asian Development Bank and Pollination.

[8] See *Part B, Chapter 1: Introductory Provisions, Section 1.3.2—Carbon Credit* of this blueprint.

INTERNATIONAL EXAMPLE

Indonesia's carbon credit regulations clearly distinguish between carbon exchanges and the domestically established registry. The regulations define the registry as a "web-based data and information management system on actions and resources for Climate Change Mitigation, Climate Change Adaptation, and [the] Economic Value of Carbon (*Nilai Ekonomi Karbon* or NEK) in Indonesia." It is separate from a "carbon exchange," which is defined as "a system that regulates the registry of carbon stocks, Carbon Trading, and the ownership status of Carbon Units."[a]

The regulations envisage that this carbon exchange could be separate from the National Registry System for Climate Change (*Sistem Registri Nasional Perubahan Iklim* or SRN PPI) and act as a trading platform for carbon units.

[a] Government of Indonesia. *Regulation of the President of the Republic of Indonesia No. 98 of 2021 on the Implementation of Carbon Pricing to Achieve the Nationally Determined Contribution Target and Control Over Greenhouse Gas Emissions in National Development.* Article 1.

Source: ADB and Pollination.

Regulating the process for transferring carbon credits is particularly important for ADB DMCs that choose to establish their own carbon crediting schemes and associated credits. However, it is always crucial to consider how such transfers interact with domestic laws and Article 6 of the Paris Agreement. From a regulatory perspective, there are two key aspects to address in relation to the transfer of carbon credits: (i) the mechanics of the transfer process itself, and (ii) any applicable restrictions or conditions on transfer. ADB DMCs must likewise ensure that credit transfers do not give rise to double counting.

4.4.1 Transfer Process

The process of transferring carbon credits generally occurs within or between carbon credit registries. For ADB DMCs relying on international crediting standards, the rules of the registries used by those standards will govern the transfer process.

On the other hand, ADB DMCs that intend to establish their own domestic carbon crediting scheme and corresponding registry will need to develop specific rules and processes governing credit transfers, in parallel with the design and functionality of the registry itself. These rules may include defining the documentation required to initiate a transfer, the steps for recording and tracking the transfer in the registry, and the authority responsible for managing the transfer process. For the actual transfer of credits between registry accounts, it is considered best practice to remove the credit entry from the first account and create a corresponding entry in the recipient's account, thereby maintaining a clear and secure chain of custody.

ADB DMCs may also wish to establish provisions regulating the interaction between domestic and international registries, including those maintained by the UNFCCC (e.g., the Article 6.4 mechanism registry) and by independent carbon standards (e.g., the Verra registry). This includes defining the process for transferring carbon credits from a domestic registry to an external one. For instance, where domestic and international registries are not directly linked, ADB DMCs could require that credits be cancelled in the originating registry and then re-issued in the destination registry to effectuate the transfer. Such international transfers may be subject to specific conditions or restrictions, as discussed in *Part B, Chapter 4: Carbon Credits, Section 4.4.2—Transfer Conditions and Restrictions.*

In designing legal frameworks that facilitate the transfer of carbon credits, ADB DMCs should consider the implications for domestic laws governing the sale and transfer of property rights, financial products and exchanges, and taxation. Where necessary, amendments to these laws may be required to ensure consistency with the carbon credit framework. ADB DMCs might also consider legal reforms that encourage participation in carbon markets, such as the introduction of tax incentives.

To promote liquidity and legal certainty in carbon markets, ADB DMCs may also consider including provisions in their legal frameworks affirming that the principle of "innocent acquirer" applies to proprietary rights in carbon credits.[9]

4.4.2 Transfer Conditions and Restrictions

ADB DMCs may also consider including restrictions or conditions on the transfer of carbon credits generated within their jurisdiction, whether such credits are recorded in a national or international registry. This is particularly important for ADB DMCs seeking compliance with Article 6 of the Paris Agreement, especially the requirements related to authorization and corresponding adjustments (see *Part B, Chapter 5: Article 6 Requirements* of this blueprint). ADB DMCs may likewise consider integrating authorization and corresponding adjustment procedures into their project approval and credit transfer processes.

In particular, ADB DMCs should carefully assess whether to permit the international transfer of domestically issued units. Any authorization for international transfer should be subject to clearly defined eligibility criteria that reflect the ADB DMC's national priorities and objectives for engaging in cooperative approaches under Article 6. This is essential to avoid potential negative impacts—such as overselling—that could undermine the achievement of the country's NDC.[10]

4.4.3 Cancellation and Retirement

Cancellation refers to the permanent removal of a carbon credit from circulation, preventing it from being traded, sold, or reused. Carbon credits are usually cancelled by updating the registry in which the credits are held.

ADB DMCs that establish their own transactional registries to support a domestic carbon crediting scheme should consider including provisions regulating when the registry operator may cancel carbon credits. Cancellation may occur in a number of circumstances, including:

(i) **where there is a "reversal"** of the outcomes achieved by the carbon crediting project;

[9] The "innocent acquirer" principle protects purchasers who acquire property for value, in good faith and without knowledge of the other party's claims to the credits. An ADB DMC's legal framework could provide clarity on what constitutes "good faith" and specify the conditions under which a purchaser may claim protection under this rule. This is discussed in the draft UNIDROIT principles on the legal nature of verified carbon credits. It is important to note that the innocent acquirer rule applies only once carbon credits exist—it does not extend to the proper acquisition of the underlying carbon rights prior to issuance.

[10] Additional guidance on Article 6 participation is provided in *Part B, Chapter 5: Article 6 Requirements* of this blueprint.

(ii) **where an error is identified** in the issuance of carbon credits (sometimes referred to as "revocation");[11] or

(iii) **upon the "retirement"** of the carbon credits.[12]

When designing provisions related to cancellation, ADB DMCs should carefully evaluate the potential impact on market participants—particularly purchasers—who may be affected by the removal of credits. This is especially important in cases involving reversals or revocation (see points (i) and (ii) above). In such circumstances, ADB DMCs could explore alternative approaches to mitigate negative impacts. For example, they might establish buffer pools to address reversals, and/or require project developers to relinquish carbon credits or procure replacement credits from the market.[13]

On the other hand, retirement occurs when an entity chooses to use carbon credits—such as for offsetting purposes—and the credits are marked as "retired" in the registry. This status, recorded in the relevant transactional registry, ensures that the credits cannot be used or claimed by another party to make a different offsetting claim. Retirement thus mitigates the risk of double counting and double claiming, making it a crucial element in supporting the integrity of a carbon crediting scheme and the effective operation of the scheme's registry.

INTERNATIONAL EXAMPLE

In Australia, Australian Carbon Credit Units (ACCUs) are held and transferred within the Australian National Registry of Emissions Units. The Clean Energy Regulator (CER), which administers the ACCU scheme, operates this registry under the Australian National Registry of Emissions Units Act 2011. Under this act, a registered ACCU holder may submit an electronic notice requesting the Clean Energy Regulator to cancel a specific ACCU. The notice must identify the ACCU to be cancelled and the registry account number in which it is held. Upon receiving the notice, the Clean Energy Regulator must remove the entry for the unit from the holder's registry account.[a]

The draft International Institute for the Unification of Private Law (UNIDROIT) principles on the legal nature of verified carbon credits also discuss the retirement of verified carbon credits, which may serve as a useful reference for Asian Development Bank (ADB) developing member countries (DMCs) developing retirement-related rules.[b] However, these principles do not address the process for initiating and processing retirement requests or how retirements should be reflected in the registry. These details would need to be defined in the ADB DMC's legal framework or implementing guidelines and procedures.

[a] Government of Australia. *Australian National Registry of Emissions Units Act 2011*. Section 64B.

[b] UNIDROIT. 2025. Draft UNIDROIT Principles on the Legal Nature of Verified Carbon Credits. Note that the principles are still in draft form and are subject to ongoing discussion.

Source: ADB and Pollination.

[11] See *Part B, Chapter 4: Carbon Credits, Section 4.2.1—Process for Issuing Credits* of this blueprint.

[12] The draft UNIDROIT principles on the legal nature of verified carbon credits include a draft principle addressing the cancellation of carbon credits. This may serve as a useful reference for ADB DMCs in understanding the legal effect of cancellation, as well as the circumstances in which cancellation may occur. UNIDROIT. 2025. Draft UNIDROIT Principles on the Legal Nature of Verified Carbon Credits. Note that the principles are still in draft form and are subject to ongoing discussion.

[13] On the use of buffer pools, see *Part B, Chapter 3: Carbon Crediting Projects, Section 3.4.2—Permanence* of this blueprint. On relinquishment or replacement, see *Part B, Chapter 7: Monitoring and Enforcement, Section 7.3.1.3—Relinquishment*.

ADB DMCs establishing their own transactional registries should consider including provisions that allow account holders to retire credits, outline the process for doing so (e.g., through an application to the registry operator), and specify how retirement is reflected in the registry. Registries may also be designed to indicate the purpose of retirement (e.g., whether credits are retired for voluntary or compliance purposes), which can enhance market data quality and the transparency of claims.

E Smart Bangkok Mass Rapid Transit Electric Ferries Project. Operating 27 fully electric ferries along 30 kilometers of the Chao Phraya River, the project supports Thailand's push for renewable transport and cleaner urban air. Environmental benefits increase when charging uses renewable energy (photo by Somkiat Jaraspat/ADB).

An airplane wing during flight. The Carbon Offsetting and Reduction Scheme for International Aviation (CORSIA) is a global market-based scheme developed by the International Civil Aviation Organization (ICAO) to address carbon dioxide emissions from international flights. It aims to stabilize international aviation's net carbon dioxide emissions at 2019 levels from 2021 onward, by requiring airlines to offset any emissions growth above a set baseline through the purchase of eligible carbon credits. As of 1 January 2025, 129 ICAO member states were voluntarily participating in CORSIA's First Phase, which runs from 2024 to 2026. The scheme will become mandatory for most ICAO member states in its Second Phase, beginning in 2027, except for exempted states such as least developed countries, small island developing states, and landlocked developing countries, unless they opt in voluntarily (photo by Simon Maage/Unsplash).

CHAPTER 5

ARTICLE 6 REQUIREMENTS

Article 6 of the Paris Agreement facilitates voluntary cooperation between countries, including through the use of market-based mechanisms, to support the achievement of their nationally determined contributions (NDCs). To participate in Article 6 cooperative approaches, governments must establish national frameworks and processes to operationalize their involvement and comply with United Nations Framework Convention on Climate Change (UNFCCC) requirements. Codifying these processes, at least in part through domestic legislation or regulation, can provide a clear and consistent regulatory environment that offers market participants guidance on critical aspects of carbon markets and their operation within an ADB DMC. Legal frameworks also enhance transparency and support regulatory alignment across regions, helping to promote private investment and facilitate cross-border transactions.

Figure 12 maps out the building blocks and their respective constituent elements for provisions governing Article 6 participation.

Figure 12: Article 6 Requirements—Building Blocks and Constituent Elements

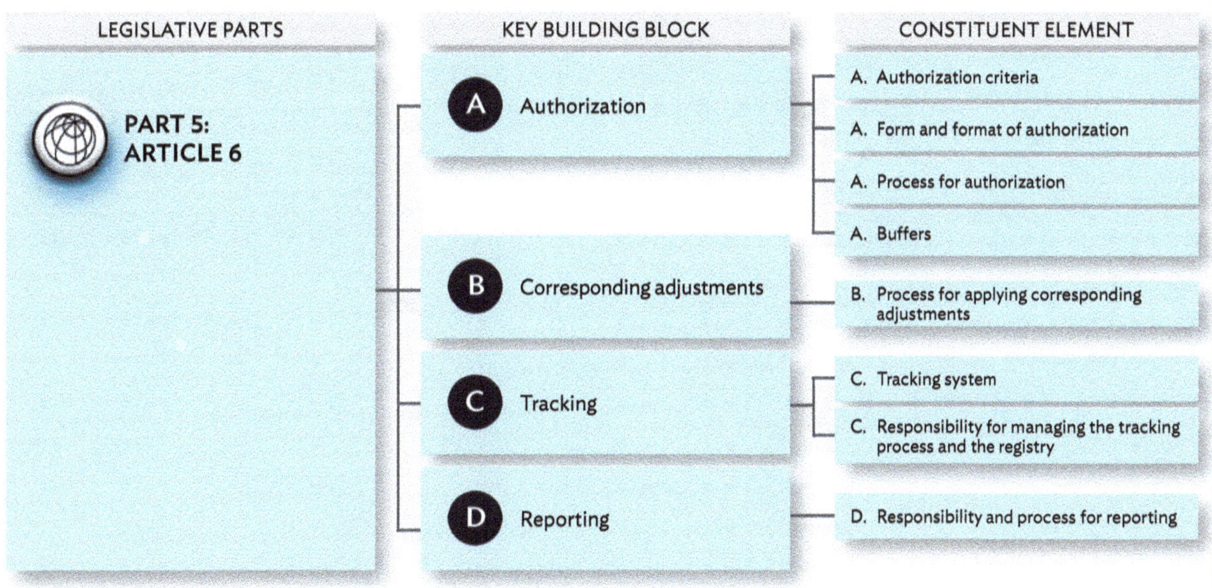

Source: Figure developed for this blueprint by the Asian Development Bank and Pollination.

These DMCs should also consider developing an Article 6 participation strategy, as part of their broader carbon market strategy and national objectives.[1] This strategy should be developed in parallel with any national legal and regulatory frameworks for Article 6 participation, to ensure alignment with the ADB DMC's policy objectives. Further guidance on assessing whether and how to engage in Article 6 cooperative approaches is provided in ADB's 2023 report, *National Strategies for Carbon Markets Under the Paris Agreement—Making Informed Policy Choices.*[2]

Table 8 summarizes the fundamental building blocks likely to be required for provisions on Article 6 participation, with building blocks related to domestic carbon crediting schemes shown on the left, and those related to international carbon crediting standards on the right.

Table 8: Participation in Cooperative Approaches Under Article 6 of the Paris Agreement—Fundamental Building Blocks Likely to Be Required

FUNDAMENTAL BUILDING BLOCKS LIKELY TO BE REQUIRED	
ADB DMC Establishing a Domestic Carbon Crediting Scheme	**ADB DMC Utilizing International Carbon Crediting Standards**
✓ Framework for authorizing ITMOs, including: - Setting national criteria for authorization (while not a strict requirement of international Article 6 rules and guidance, this is recommended to enhance the integrity of the ADB DMC's Article 6 approach); - Establishing the contents and format for authorization, aligned with the international Article 6 rules and guidance;[a] and - Defining the process for authorization (including how to apply for authorization, who will assess and approve applications, and any other procedural requirements).	✓ Framework for authorizing ITMOs, including: - Setting national criteria for authorization (while not a strict requirement of international Article 6 rules and guidance, this is recommended to enhance the integrity of the ADB DMC's Article 6 approach); - Establishing the contents and format for authorization that align with the international Article 6 rules and guidance;[a] and - Defining the process for authorization (including how to apply for authorization, who will assess and approve applications, and any other procedural requirements).
✓ Process for applying corresponding adjustments.	✓ Process for applying corresponding adjustments.
✓ Establishment of an Article 6-compliant tracking system, which will likely be the national scheme registry (see *Part B, Chapter 4: Carbon Credits, Section 4.3—Registration of Carbon Credits* of this blueprint). ADB DMCs establishing a national scheme registry should ensure that it is capable of tracking information related to ITMOs, as set out in the Article 6 rules and guidance (see *Part B, Chapter 5: Article 6 Requirements, Section 5.4—Key Building Block C: Tracking* of this blueprint).	✓ Establishment of an Article 6-compliant tracking system, which may involve one or a combination of the following approaches: (i) establishing a national informational registry, (ii) using a UNFCCC-operated international registry, (iii) drawing upon international scheme registries (noting that the PACM will have its own mechanism registry to record and track authorized Article 6.4 emissions reductions), or (iv) a hybrid of these approaches. In doing so, ADB DMCs should also consider which entity will be responsible for maintaining and updating the registry, and how that entity will obtain the information to be recorded.

continued on next page

[1] See *Part A: Introduction and Background* of this blueprint.

[2] ADB. 2023. National Strategies for Carbon Markets under the Paris Agreement—Making Informed Policy Choices.

Table 8 *continued*

FUNDAMENTAL BUILDING BLOCKS LIKELY TO BE REQUIRED	
ADB DMC Establishing a Domestic Carbon Crediting Scheme	**ADB DMC Utilizing International Carbon Crediting Standards**
✓ Responsibility and processes for preparing and submitting Article 6-related reports to the UNFCCC, in accordance with the Article 6 rules and guidance.	✓ Responsibility and processes for preparing and submitting Article 6-related reports to the UNFCCC, in accordance with the Article 6 rules and guidance.

ADB = Asian Development Bank, DMC = developing member country, ITMO = internationally transferred mitigation outcome, PACM = Paris Agreement Crediting Mechanism established under Article 6.4 of the Paris Agreement, UNFCCC = United Nations Framework Convention on Climate Change.

[a] UNFCCC, CMA. 2024. Decision 4/CMA.6. Part I, paras. 5–6.

Source: ADB and Pollination.

ADB DMCs seeking to engage in Article 6 of the Paris Agreement should take into account the evolving nature of Article 6 rules and guidance when designing their carbon market frameworks and legislation.[3] Some of the key considerations as of April 2025 are discussed elsewhere in this chapter, including (i) international transfers of mitigation outcomes (and the credits representing those outcomes), (ii) authorizations, (iii) corresponding adjustments, and (iv) reporting obligations under Article 6.

This blueprint does not provide detailed guidance on the legislative provisions required for participation in the Paris Agreement Crediting Mechanism (PACM) under Article 6.4, beyond outlining the basic participation requirements. Nevertheless, the key considerations discussed remain relevant to ADB DMCs intending to authorize Article 6.4 emission reductions (A6.4 ERs) generated and credited under the PACM in accordance with Article 6 rules and guidance.

ADB DMCs participating in Article 6 should also consider formalizing the allocation of roles and responsibilities related to their participation—along with associated processes and procedures—across relevant government departments, and establishing clear points of contact for market participants. These aspects could be addressed through the governance arrangements set out in the legal framework.[4]

5.1 Key Building Block A: Authorization

Article 6.2 of the Paris Agreement establishes a system for trading internationally transferred mitigation outcomes (ITMOs). In the context of the Paris Agreement, the term "mitigation outcomes" refers to a standardized measure of the outcome of efforts to reduce emissions from sources or enhance carbon sinks. Mitigation outcomes can include carbon credits, measured in metric tons of greenhouse gas (GHG) emissions reductions or removals, as well as other units quantified using different metrics, such as megawatt-hours of green electricity generated and used, or square kilometers of reforestation.

[3] Decisions on Article 6 at COP26 adopted guidance on cooperative approaches referred to in Article 6.2; rules, modalities, and procedures for the mechanism established by Article 6.4; and a work program under the framework for non-market approaches under Article 6.8. As this document primarily focuses on Articles 6.2 and 6.4, the unofficial phrase "Article 6 guidance and rules" is used to encompass the decisions to date on both Article 6.2 and Article 6.4.

[4] See *Part B, Chapter 2: Governance* of this blueprint.

Host countries (i.e., countries where the ITMOs are generated) may authorize credits for use toward another country's NDC or for "other international mitigation purposes," such as airline compliance under the Carbon Offsetting and Reduction Scheme for International Aviation (CORSIA). They may also authorize credits for "other mitigation purposes," which, while not explicitly defined in the Article 6 rules and guidance, is commonly interpreted to include voluntary uses of carbon credits. Authorization offers a key benefit in this context: it allows purchasers to claim full rights over the credits, knowing that the same credits are not being counted toward the host country's NDC. This clarity may increase buyer demand and the carbon credit price.

Importantly, the Article 6 rules and guidance leave it to host countries to determine whether credits used for voluntary purposes qualify as "other mitigation purposes." Therefore, while not required, ADB DMCs have the option to authorize carbon credits generated in the country for use towards voluntary purposes.

Figure 13 sets out the different pathways for treating and using a mitigation outcome under the Paris Agreement.

Figure 13: Treatment and Use of a Mitigation Outcome Under the Paris Agreement

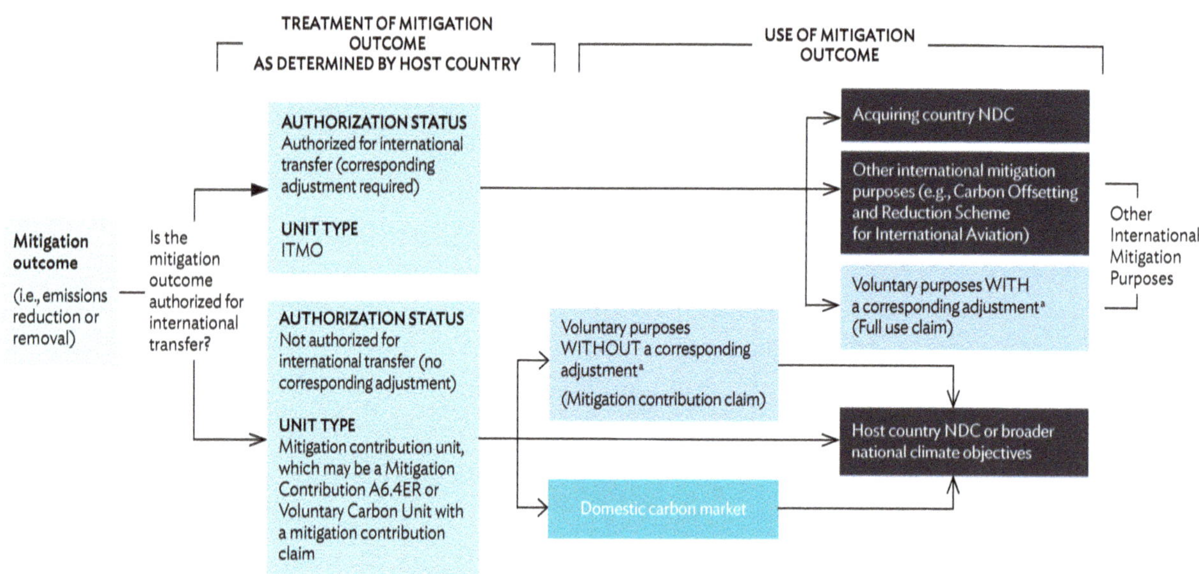

A6.4ER = Article 6.4 Emission Reduction Unit, ITMO = internationally transferred mitigation outcome, NDC = nationally determined contribution.

Note: The figure is adapted from the original version published by the Asian Development Bank (ADB) in the 2023 report National Strategies for Carbon Markets Under the Paris Agreement.

[a] It is a host country's prerogative to decide under what circumstances a mitigation outcome used for voluntary purposes requires national authorization and a corresponding adjustment.

Source: ADB and Pollination; ADB. 2023. National Strategies for Carbon Markets under the Paris Agreement—Making Informed Policy Choices. p. 7.

Establishing a robust national legal framework that sets out the authorization process—for all purposes—can help countries maximize the benefits of participating in international carbon markets in a way that aligns with their unique national circumstances and priorities. This framework can include credits generated under domestic schemes, credits generated in the country under international carbon crediting standards, and A6.4ERs generated under the PACM (footnote 2).

At COP29, parties adopted guidance on the process, timing, content, and form of authorization.[5] While host countries retain flexibility in the exact form and process of authorization, certain elements are mandatory. Most host countries are expected to issue a "Letter of Authorization" (or an equivalent document) confirming that the ITMOs specified in the letter are authorized for use toward achieving another country's NDC, for other international mitigation purposes (including voluntary purposes), or any combination of these purposes. The latest guidance also clarified the three components of authorization: (i) authorization of the cooperative approach, (ii) authorization of ITMOs, and (iii) authorization of entities.

Decisions made at COP29 provide parties with clarity on the following matters:

(i) **Authorization content.** When authorizing the use of ITMOs for cooperative approaches, parties must include the following information:
   (a) a unique identifier for the cooperative approach;
   (b) the name(s) of the participating party(ies) or entities covered by the authorization, if known;
   (c) the date and duration of the authorization, and the final date for mitigation outcomes to be issued, used, or cancelled;
   (d) the specification of the first transfer of the mitigation outcome;
   (e) the uses covered by the authorization;
   (f) the identification of underlying regulations, frameworks, standards, procedures, or specific methodologies;
   (g) information on the circumstances under which changes to authorization may occur and how double counting will be avoided;
   (h) the quantity of ITMOs;
   (i) identification of the registry used for tracking and recording ITMOs;
   (j) identification of the registry that contains mitigation outcomes (or the information used in their calculation) and transparently tracks the status of the underlying mitigation activities and outcomes, as well as participation and transactions by various entities; and
   (k) information covered by the authorization, including vintages, metrics and units of measurement, sectors, and activity types.[6]

(ii) **Format.** Parties may adopt their own format to provide the required information in authorizations. In March 2025, the UNFCCC published a voluntary template that parties may opt to use. When setting out any form or format for authorizations, ADB DMCs should consider that requirements at the international level may evolve over time. Therefore, administrative processes—such as the format of authorization—should be flexible enough to accommodate (at least annual) updates.

As parties determine how to comply with the content requirements, design preferred formats, and identify additional information to include in authorizations, ADB DMCs may wish to consider incorporating the following additional provisions:

---

5 UNFCCC, CMA. 2024. Decision 4/CMA.6. Part 1, paras. 2–10.

6 UNFCCC, CMA. 2024. Decision 4/CMA.6. Part 1, para. 5.

(i) **Authorization criteria.** These are the criteria the ADB DMC will use to assess and approve authorization applications. They should include:

  (a) **Minimum eligibility requirements under Article 6 rules and guidance**, including that ITMOs must be:
  - real, verified, and additional;
  - emissions reductions or removals;
  - measured in metric tons of carbon dioxide equivalent or in other non-GHG metrics agreed upon by the participating parties that are consistent with their respective NDCs;
  - derived from a cooperative approach under Article 6.2, or from Article 6.4 emissions reductions issued under the mechanism established by Article 6.4 (when authorized); and
  - representing mitigation from 2021 onward.[7]

  (b) **Additional criteria to align with national strategies and NDC implementation.** These may include:
  - Criteria to reflect national priorities and opportunities, such as criteria that align with the ADB DMC's sustainable development goals and its objectives in participating in Article 6 (e.g., prioritization of certain technologies or activities to facilitate sector decarbonization), and/or criteria that align with the host country's long-term low emissions development strategy or other climate strategies; and
  - Criteria to manage overselling risks, described further in *Part A: Introduction and Background* of this blueprint. These criteria could include restricting the types of activities and/or sectors which might be considered for authorization (e.g., depending on the cost of mitigation) using "positive" and/or "negative" lists. For instance, Ghana has developed a "whitelist" of mitigation activities in its conditional NDC (presumed additional if certain conditions are met), and a "red list" of mitigation activities ineligible for authorization, based on the unconditional mitigation programs of actions in its NDC.

  (c) **Pre-authorization process.** ADB DMCs could also include a process for confirming a project's eligibility for authorization at the time of registration, based on the ADB DMC's authorization eligibility criteria. This is sometimes referred to as a "pre-authorization" process.

(ii) **Process and responsibility.** This provision may include the process for issuing the authorization, including the authority or entity responsible for approving and issuing the authorization, the body responsible for conducting the underlying assessment or analysis to inform this decision, and whether stakeholder consultation will be required as part of the process.

(iii) **Measures to address overselling risks.** ADB DMCs could opt to establish a buffer system to collect a proportion of authorized mitigation outcomes. This pool of reserved credits could help the host country minimize the risk of overselling credits against its NDC target.

While most ADB DMCs are expected to be exporters of ITMOs, any ADB DMC that anticipates acquiring ITMOs generated in other countries for use toward its own NDC should consider establishing processes to facilitate the recognition and accounting of these ITMOs. These processes should include verifying that authorization has been granted by the appropriate authority of the exporting host country , and ensuring that both countries make corresponding adjustments.

7 UNFCCC, CMA. 2021. Decision 2/CMA.3. Annex. p. 5.

INTERNATIONAL EXAMPLE

Under Zambia's Green Economy and Climate Change Act, 2024, any person intending to trade carbon credits generated in Zambia must apply for a certificate of authorization from the director of green economy and climate change. The director must approve or reject the application within 30 days of receipt. To obtain a certificate of authorization, the emissions reductions or removals underpinning the carbon credits must have been verified by a registered verifier, and the project must either be approved under the same law, or the proponent must hold a carbon stock management permit issued pursuant to the Forests Act, 2015.

When deciding whether to issue the certificate, the director must consider the following in relation to the project:

(i) Preservation of environmental integrity;
(ii) Avoidance of double counting;
(iii) The participation of, and benefit-sharing with, local communities in the profits arising from carbon trading;
(iv) The project's demonstration of additionality; and
(v) Promotion of sustainable development.[a]

On the other hand, Ghana clarifies in its national Article 6 framework that it will authorize mitigation outcomes associated with conditional NDC activities, as well as activities outside the NDC. To identify which activities fall under the conditional portion of the NDC and are eligible for international transfer, Ghana has established a "whitelist" of 25 activity types, including forest conservation activities.

VCM projects aiming to generate carbon credits must obtain formal recognition to ensure enhanced accounting in reporting. The framework explicitly states that VCM projects are not required to undergo corresponding adjustments, though they may request one if desired.

The framework outlines the authorization process and how it fits into the mitigation activity development cycle. In summary, project proponents seeking authorization must:

(i) Open an account in the national registry;
(ii) Prepare a "Mitigation Activity Idea Note" (project proponents may also request a letter of assurance for pre-authorization at this stage, if the activity is included on the "whitelist"); and
(iii) Prepare a "Mitigation Activity Design Document" and provide a letter of support from the relevant line ministry.

The Carbon Market Committee will then determine whether to issue a letter of recommendation allowing the proponent to proceed to the validation stage and initiate the authorization process. Once this recommendation is granted, the project undergoes independent validation. Upon completion of validation, the project can request a letter of authorization from the Carbon Market Office, which will then prepare an "Article 6.2 Initial Report" to the UNFCCC.

Once the project outcomes have been reported and verified by an accredited entity, Ghana and the participating acquiring party will conduct a positive examination of the verification report. Following this, the authorized and verified carbon credits may be issued in the registry.[b]

NDC = nationally determined contribution, UNFCCC = United Nations Framework Convention on Climate Change, VCM = voluntary carbon market.

[a] Government of Zambia. 2024. *Green Economy and Climate Change Act, 2024*. Sections 23 and 24.

[b] Government of Ghana. 2022. *Ghana's Framework on International Carbon Markets and Non-Market Approaches*. Schedule 2.

Source: Asian Development Bank and Pollination.

As ADB DMCs move forward with authorization, they should keep in mind that authorizations for the use of ITMOs may be subject to change. However, such changes cannot affect mitigation outcomes that have already undergone a first transfer, unless otherwise agreed by the participating parties. In line with the authorization requirements, ADB DMCs should carefully consider the circumstances under which changes may occur, the mechanisms in place to avoid double counting, and the potential implications these changes may have on securing cooperative approach transactions.

5.2 Key Building Block B: Corresponding Adjustments

To ensure transparency and prevent double counting under Article 6 of the Paris Agreement, host countries must apply a "corresponding adjustment" by adding the number of mitigation outcomes authorized for international transfer to their NDC emissions balance. Conversely, the acquiring country must apply a corresponding adjustment in the opposite direction by subtracting the same number of mitigation outcomes from its own NDC emissions balance.

Figure 14 illustrates this principle. In this example, Country A achieves 50 mitigation outcomes during a given NDC period and has exceeded its NDC target.[8] Country B seeks to use ITMOs acquired from another country to help meet its own NDC target. If Country A transfers 30 ITMOs to Country B, it must apply a corresponding adjustment by adding 30 to its NDC emissions balance—raising it from 50 to 80. Conversely, Country B must subtract 30 from its own NDC emissions balance—reducing it from 100 to 70.

This accounting system helps mitigate the risk of double counting, where two different entities might use the same ITMOs to meet their Paris Agreement targets. ADB DMCs that choose to engage in Article 6 cooperative approaches will be required to regularly report to the UNFCCC, including details on authorizations and corresponding adjustments.

Approaches to applying corresponding adjustments under Article 6 are still being finalized at the international level. Currently, there are two options available, depending on the structure of a party's NDC target. Countries with a multi-year target are required to use the multi-year trajectory approach. In contrast, countries with a single-year target may choose between the multi-year trajectory approach and the averaging approach (Table 9).[9]

It is recommended that ADB DMCs avoid specifying the exact approach for applying corresponding adjustments in legislation. Instead, legal frameworks could refer more generally to alignment with international rules and guidance on corresponding adjustments, as these are agreed. However, ADB DMCs should clearly define which authority or body is responsible for determining when corresponding adjustments must be applied and for implementing these adjustments as part of the DMC's Article 6 accounting and reporting obligations.

8 Country A does not need to wait until it has achieved or exceeded its NDC targets before pursuing opportunities to finance mitigation outcomes through carbon trading.

9 UNFCCC, CMA. 2021. Decision 2/CMA.3. Part III, para. 7(a).

Figure 14: Corresponding Adjustment Under Article 6

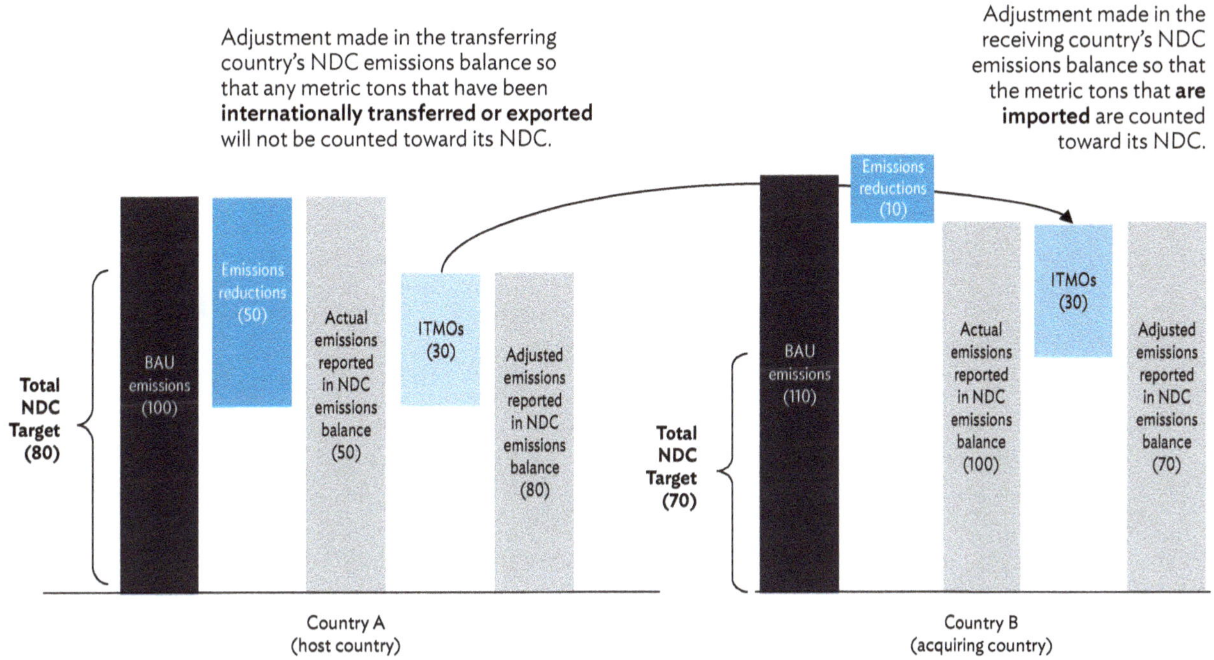

BAU = business-as-usual, GHG = greenhouse gas, ITMO = internationally transferred mitigation outcome, NDC = nationally determined contribution.

Note: The figure is adapted from the original version published by the Asian Development Bank (ADB) in the 2023 report National Strategies for Carbon Markets under the Paris Agreement, with further refinements to reflect the latest Article 6 rules and guidance agreed upon during COP29.

Source: Figure developed by ADB and Pollination. ADB. 2023. National Strategies for Carbon Markets under the Paris Agreement—Making Informed Policy Choices. p. 8.

Table 9: Approaches to Applying Corresponding Adjustments

APPROACH	DESCRIPTION
Averaging Approach	• This approach can be used by countries with a single-year target NDC (e.g., X% reductions by 2030). • Under this approach, countries "calculate the average annual amount of ITMOs first transferred and used over the NDC implementation period by taking the cumulative amount and dividing by the number of elapsed years in the NDC implementation period."[a] • Under this approach, an NDC target is either achieved or not based on the final result.
Trajectory Approach	• This approach can be used by countries with either a single-year target or a multi-year NDC target (e.g., X% reductions between 2021 and 2030). • Under this approach, ITMOs are accounted for every year. • The ADB DMC must also comply with the reporting requirements regarding corresponding adjustments (see *Part B, Chapter 5: Article 6 Requirements, Section 5.5—Key Building Block D: Reporting* of this blueprint).

ADB = Asian Development Bank, DMC = developing member country, ITMO = internationally transferred mitigation outcome, NDC = nationally determined contribution.

[a] Oxford Climate Policy. 2022. *Pocket Guide to Article 6 Under the Paris Agreement*. p. 23.

Source: ADB and Pollination.

ADB DMCs may also consider publicly disclosing their approach to applying corresponding adjustments to enhance market transparency. In addition, parties must communicate their chosen method for applying corresponding adjustments in the Article 6.2 initial report, which is required upon authorization of ITMOs from a cooperative approach.[10]

5.3 Key Building Block C: Tracking

5.3.1 Tracking System

In addition, ADB DMCs will need to establish the necessary tracking capacity and infrastructure for participation in Article 6, as discussed in *Part B, Chapter 4: Carbon Credits, Section 4.3—Key Building Block B: Registration of Carbon Credits* of this blueprint.

Broadly, there are three types of registries that ADB DMCs may use for Article 6 tracking purposes:

(i) National registries established by the host country;

(ii) The international registry to be established by the UNFCCC by 2025;[11] and

(iii) Registries established by independent carbon crediting bodies (e.g., the Verra registry) and the Article 6.4 mechanism registry.

These registries can be used in a complementary manner. For example, an ADB DMC may rely on the registry of an independent crediting scheme—or, in the case of participation in the PACM, the Article 6.4 mechanism registry—for managing the transactional aspects. The DMC could then use its national registry to compile and organize relevant data from these registries for Article 6 tracking and reporting purposes.

It is important to note that parties to the Paris Agreement are subject to specific reporting obligations under the UNFCCC, which require certain types of information regarding the projects and the ITMOs authorized. Registries of international crediting schemes may not contain all the required data. In such cases, ADB DMCs will need to obtain the necessary information through other means, such as requiring project proponents to provide documentation during the project approval and authorization process.[12]

The approach taken will depend on each ADB DMC's institutional capacity and available resources. Digitalized, interoperable national registries can enhance the integrity of a country's Article 6 approach and strengthen buyer confidence in its ITMOs. However, developing and maintaining such registry systems may require substantial financial, technical, and human resources. For ADB DMCs with limited resources, it may be more practical to leverage the infrastructure of international registries managed by the UNFCCC or by international carbon crediting programs.

10 UNFCCC, CMA. 2021. Decision 2/CMA.3. Part IV, para. 18(c).

11 In addition to tracking services, the international registry can also provide issuance services for parties that request them.

12 While parties will need to track information required for reporting, they may choose to continue using the transactional infrastructure of third-party registries, including international crediting mechanisms and the international registry established under Article 6.4, if it includes transactional capabilities.

INTERNATIONAL EXAMPLE

In its national Article 6 framework, Ghana has established a national carbon registry—the Ghana Carbon Registry—to support compliance with Article 6 tracking requirements. The framework outlines the registry's core functions and specifies that its technical and administrative management will be based on secure software capable of tracking and recording ITMOs. It also includes provisions for labeling ITMOs, such as the use of unique serial numbers, to ensure traceability.

The framework provides detailed guidance on registry operations, including account opening, information registration, and the issuance of ITMOs. It also acknowledges that carbon crediting projects may be registered under international carbon crediting standards. In such cases, where Ghana authorizes ITMOs to be issued through an international standard's registry, the administrator of that registry must provide the Carbon Market Office with issuance information no later than 7 days after issuance.[a]

ITMO = internationally transferred mitigation outcome.

[a] Government of Ghana. 2022. *Ghana's Framework on International Carbon Markets and Non-Market Approaches*. Schedule 8.

Source: Asian Development Bank and Pollination.

5.3.2 Responsibility for Managing the Tracking Process and Registry

When establishing national tracking processes to align with Article 6 participation requirements, ADB DMCs will need to determine which entity will be responsible for maintaining and updating the tracking system. This includes setting out the process for obtaining information from project proponents and other registries—such as transactional registries used by independent carbon crediting schemes or the Article 6.4 mechanism registry—regarding the first transfer and use or cancellation of ITMOs.

5.3.3 Information That Is Tracked

The Article 6 rules and guidance require participating parties to have, or have access to, a registry to track ITMOs.[13]

The registry must:

(i) have accounts for ITMOs, as necessary;

(ii) record actions related to ITMOs, including authorization, first transfer, transfer, acquisition, use toward NDCs, authorization for use toward other international mitigation purposes, and voluntary cancellation (including for overall mitigation in global emissions, if applicable);

(iii) track, maintain records, and account for ITMOs, including through the use of unique identifiers;

(iv) provide access to the ADB DMC and other entities authorized by the ADB DMC to implement the actions referred to in (ii); and

(v) generate, maintain, and compile records, information, and data in line with the annual reporting requirements under the Article 6 rules and guidance, using the agreed electronic format.

[13] UNFCCC, CMA. 2021. Decision 2/CMA.3. Annex, Part VI, para. 29.

ADB DMCs should design their tracking systems to comply with these requirements and to facilitate the proper tracking of ITMOs generated domestically, as well as those acquired internationally for use toward the ADB DMC's NDC.

5.4 Key Building Block D: Reporting

Parties participating in Article 6 are required to regularly report their Article 6 activities to the UNFCCC. This includes submission of the Article 6.2 initial report, annual information, and inputs to the Biennial Transparency Report. Reporting must cover authorizations issued and corresponding adjustments applied by the party.

ADB DMCs participating in Article 6 should thus designate a relevant governance body or minister to monitor international developments on Article 6 reporting guidance and ensure timely reporting to the UNFCCC.

ADB DMCs should also design their tracking systems (including any national registry) to collect the data needed for Article 6 reporting. This entails identifying the information that must be provided by project proponents to support compliance with reporting requirements.

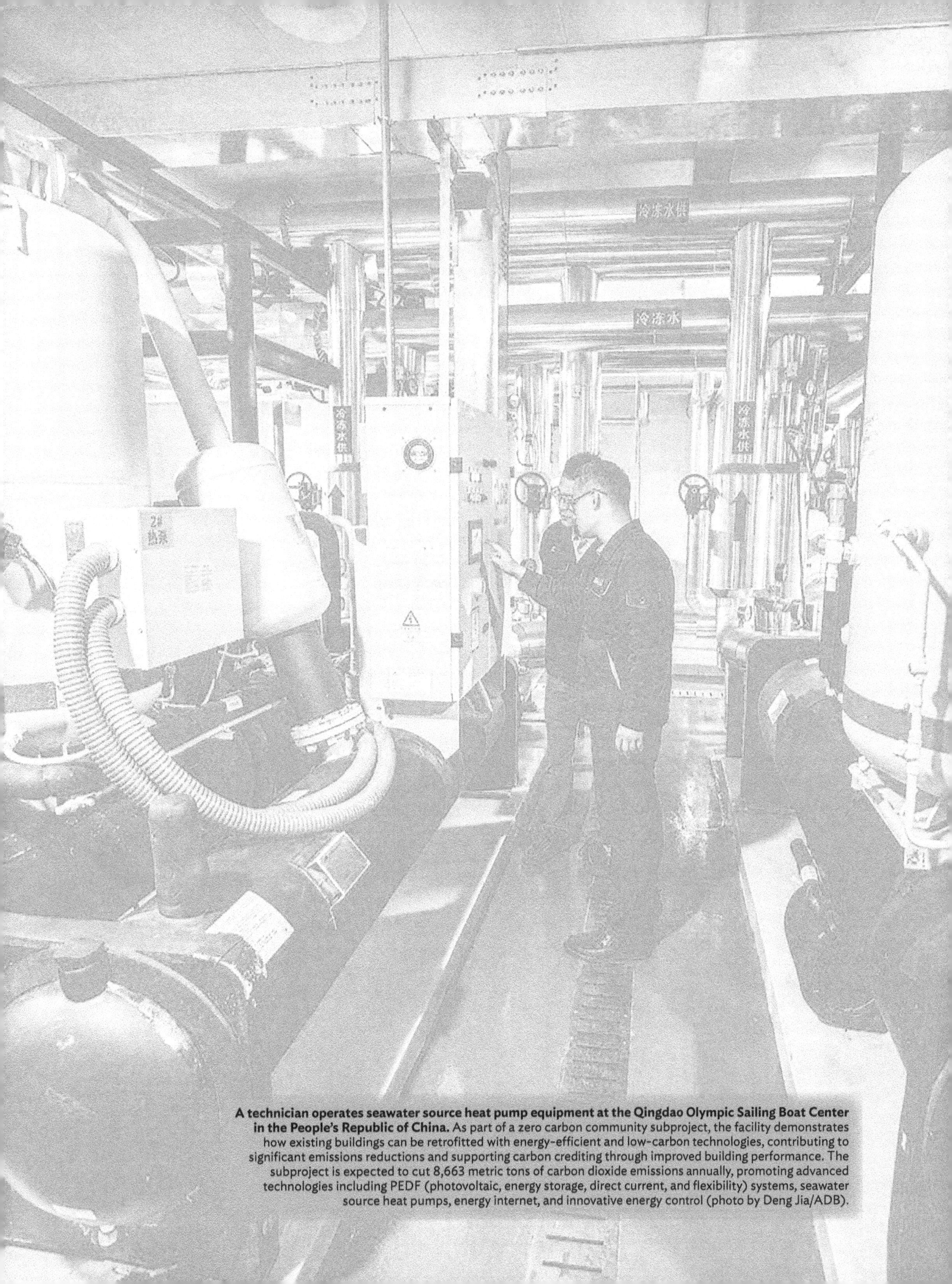

A technician operates seawater source heat pump equipment at the Qingdao Olympic Sailing Boat Center in the People's Republic of China. As part of a zero carbon community subproject, the facility demonstrates how existing buildings can be retrofitted with energy-efficient and low-carbon technologies, contributing to significant emissions reductions and supporting carbon crediting through improved building performance. The subproject is expected to cut 8,663 metric tons of carbon dioxide emissions annually, promoting advanced technologies including PEDF (photovoltaic, energy storage, direct current, and flexibility) systems, seawater source heat pumps, energy internet, and innovative energy control (photo by Deng Jia/ADB).

An electronics engineer checks vehicle software with their team. Engineering plays a key role in cutting vehicle emissions through electrification, hybrid systems, aerodynamic design, and more efficient engines (photo by ThisisEngineering/Unsplash).

CHAPTER 6

SOCIAL AND ENVIRONMENTAL SAFEGUARDS

Social and environmental safeguards are needed to ensure that projects deliver positive outcomes for local communities and ecosystems. These include general safeguards and safeguards concerning Indigenous Peoples and local communities (Figure 15).

Figure 15: Social and Environmental Safeguards—Building Blocks and Constituent Elements

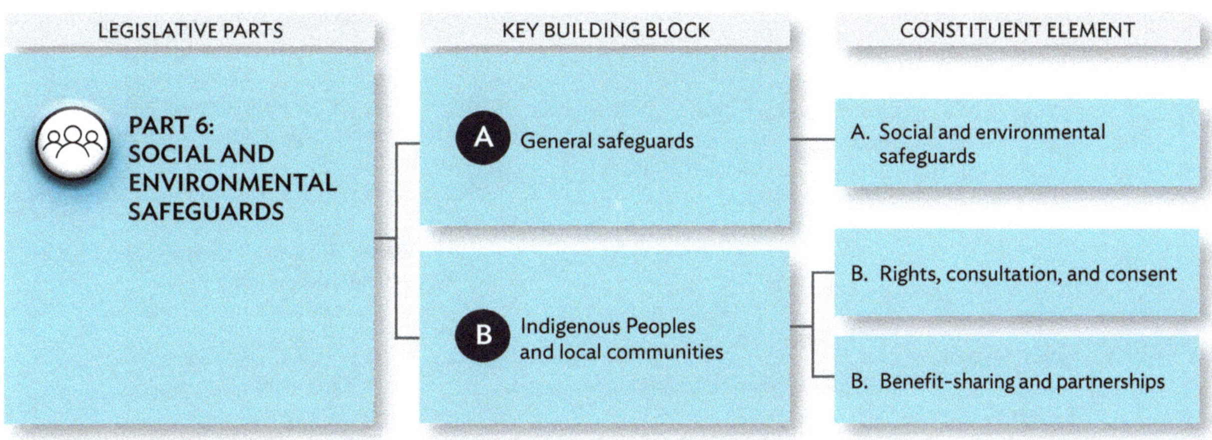

Source: Figure developed for this blueprint by the Asian Development Bank and Pollination.

6.1 Summary of Fundamental Building Blocks Likely to Be Required

Table 10 summarizes the fundamental building blocks likely to be required for provisions concerning social and environmental safeguards, with building blocks relating to domestic carbon crediting schemes shown on the left, and those relating to international carbon crediting standards on the right.

Table 10: Social and Environmental Safeguards—Fundamental Building Blocks Likely to Be Required

FUNDAMENTAL BUILDING BLOCKS LIKELY TO BE REQUIRED	
ADB DMC Establishing a Domestic Carbon Crediting Scheme	**ADB DMC Utilizing International Carbon Crediting Standards**
✓ Social and environmental safeguards, including measures to: - Respect rights, including human rights and protections under international and national law; - Align projects with domestic environmental, social, and economic regulations; - Enhance sustainable development outcomes; - Protect and uphold the rights of Indigenous Peoples and local communities, including the right to free, prior, and informed consent (FPIC); and - Prevent adverse environmental impacts from carbon crediting projects.	✓ International carbon crediting schemes (including the PACM) often incorporate safeguards within their standards. However, ADB DMCs should still consider adopting safeguards tailored to their domestic context, including measures to: - Respect rights, including human rights and protections under international and national law; - Align projects with domestic environmental, social, and economic regulations; - Enhance sustainable development outcomes; - Protect and uphold the rights of Indigenous Peoples and local communities, including the right to free, prior, and informed consent (FPIC); and - Prevent adverse environmental impacts from carbon crediting projects.
✓ Safeguards relating to Indigenous Peoples and local communities, including: - Protection of their rights, such as the right to FPIC; and - Inclusion of Indigenous Peoples and local communities as core partners in carbon crediting projects conducted on lands they steward or where they maintain an active relationship.	✓ While international carbon crediting schemes often include requirements related to engagement with Indigenous Peoples and local communities, these are not always consistent or necessarily appropriate for the ADB DMC's domestic context. ADB DMCs should therefore strongly consider including their own safeguards, including: - Protecting the rights of Indigenous Peoples and local communities (such as the right to FPIC); and - Ensuring their inclusion as core partners in carbon crediting projects conducted on lands they steward or where they maintain an active relationship.

ADB = Asian Development Bank; DMC = developing member country; FPIC = free, prior, and informed consent; PACM = Paris Agreement Crediting Mechanism established under Article 6.4 of the Paris Agreement.
Source: ADB and Pollination.

6.2 Key Building Block A: General Safeguards

Social and environmental safeguards are essential to ensure the full and equitable participation of all stakeholders—including Indigenous Peoples and local communities—in carbon crediting projects, and to mitigate the risk of net negative social or environmental impacts. ADB DMCs should strongly consider incorporating provisions on such safeguards within their carbon crediting legal frameworks.

Some international carbon crediting standards, such as the Paris Agreement Crediting Mechanism established under Article 6.4 of the Paris Agreement (PACM), have safeguards built into their standards. For example, the PACM utilizes a sustainable development tool that mandates project proponents to assess and mitigate the risk of their projects infringing upon various social and environmental safeguards. However, these safeguards may not always be appropriately tailored to an ADB DMC's domestic context. There is also considerable variation in the level and scope of safeguards across different international carbon crediting schemes.

For this reason, safeguards should be applied consistently, whether the ADB DMC is developing a domestic carbon crediting scheme or participating in international schemes. These safeguards should, at a minimum, ensure that projects meet the baseline requirements outlined in Figure 16.

Figure 16: Minimum Safeguards

Source: Figure developed for this blueprint by the Asian Development Bank and Pollination.

ADB DMCs could consider including the following elements in their carbon crediting legal frameworks:

(i) **A requirement for project proponents to comply with applicable domestic and/or international environmental, social, and economic regulations**. This serves as a minimum "catch-all" requirement; however, additional, more specific safeguards are strongly recommended.

(ii) **A requirement for project proponents to demonstrate compliance with relevant international and domestic frameworks and regulations on the recognition, respect, and protection of human rights**. This could include describing how the project aligns with applicable human rights standards and protections, and outlining the mechanisms—such as partnerships, grievance procedures, or appeals processes—established to safeguard the rights of project participants, stakeholders, and affected communities.

(iii) **Provisions specific to projects conducted on land stewarded by Indigenous Peoples and local communities, or land to which they have legal, traditional, and/or customary claims**.[1] This includes requirements to uphold the right to ongoing free, prior and informed consent (FPIC).

(iv) **A requirement for project proponents to describe how the project contributes to the ADB DMC's sustainable development goals and other relevant domestic policies**. This could form part of the project approval and registration process. Proponents could also be required to undergo third-party environmental and social impact assessments.

(v) **The development of clear liability regimes to address harms to the environment and human health**.

ADB DMCs should determine which government entity will be responsible for collecting information and monitoring project compliance with social and environmental safeguards. This will typically be the entity administering the carbon crediting legal framework, with consideration given to its

[1] See *Part B, Chapter 6: Social and Environmental Safeguards, Section 6.3—Key Building Block B: Indigenous Peoples and Local Communities: Rights and Partnerships* of this blueprint.

capability and capacity to carry out effective oversight. ADB DMCs should also consider requiring that compliance with the legal framework—and with any applicable independent carbon crediting standard—be independently validated and verified, as discussed in *Part B, Chapter 7: Monitoring and Enforcement, Section 7.2.1—Monitoring, Reporting, and Verification, Recordkeeping and Audit Requirements* of this blueprint.

INTERNATIONAL EXAMPLE

Tanzania's carbon market regulations require carbon crediting projects to demonstrate community involvement; adopt transparent and fair business practices; align with national investment priorities; implement benefit-sharing mechanisms; and adhere to ecological, social, cultural, and economic safeguards, including corporate social responsibility.[a] Projects must also undergo environmental and social impact assessments in accordance with Tanzania's Environmental Impact Assessment Regulations.[b] Furthermore, where a carbon trading project causes damage, the person who installed the project or the project proponent who permitted it to be installed is liable for the damage caused to environmental or human health, as provided under domestic law.[c] Finally, local government authorities are tasked with safeguarding the interests of local communities involved in carbon trading projects and programs.[d]

[a] Government of Tanzania. 2023. *The Environmental Management (Control and Management of Carbon Trading Regulations) 2022*, as amended by *The Environmental Management (Control and Management of Carbon Trading) (Amendment) Regulations, 2023*. Regulation 24.
[b] Footnote a, Regulation 25.
[c] Footnote a, Regulation 44.
[d] Footnote a, Regulation 17(c).
Source: Asian Development Bank and Pollination.

6.3 Key Building Block B: Indigenous Peoples and Local Communities—Rights and Partnerships

Discussions around the involvement of Indigenous Peoples and local communities in carbon markets have often focused on two distinct but interrelated concepts: rights (including consent and consultation) and benefit-sharing.

6.3.1 Rights, Consultation, and Consent

At a minimum, countries must ensure that the rights and knowledge of Indigenous Peoples and local communities are appropriately protected. This includes, most fundamentally, the right to FPIC (see *Part B, Chapter 3: Carbon Crediting Projects, Section 3.2.3—Consents from Third Parties with Legal Interests in Land* of this blueprint).[2]

[2] See the *United Nations Declaration on the Rights of Indigenous Peoples*, which was adopted by the United Nations General Assembly in 2007.

In addition to safeguarding rights related to land and territories, carbon crediting projects may seek to use or draw upon indigenous knowledge, such as indigenous ecological knowledge. Under international law, Indigenous Peoples have the right to maintain, control, protect, and develop their cultural heritage, traditional knowledge, and traditional cultural expressions, including associated intellectual property.[3] ADB DMCs should thus ensure these rights are protected, including the right to FPIC for any use of such knowledge.

Furthermore, ADB DMCs can help create an enabling environment in which these rights are consistently respected and upheld. One way to do this is by promoting partnership and "shareholdership" models between non-indigenous project proponents and Indigenous Peoples, rather than relying solely on transactional, consent-focused approaches, as discussed in the following sections.

6.3.2 Benefit-Sharing and Partnerships

In the context of carbon markets, benefits refer to "any gain to stakeholders resulting from the carbon [crediting] project," including "both monetary payments and non-monetary benefits."[4] Benefit-sharing arrangements define how these benefits are allocated and distributed among project participants and other stakeholders, such as local communities. Benefit-sharing can involve a wide range of participants, including Indigenous Peoples, local communities, and national or local governments.

This section focuses on benefit-sharing as a mechanism specifically used to engage Indigenous Peoples and local communities. Approaches to benefit-sharing and engagement with these groups have evolved over time, ranging from highly transactional models to more transformational approaches, as illustrated in Figure 17.

Historically, carbon markets have emphasized benefit-sharing and transaction-based approaches. However, there is a shift toward "equity-sharing" and shareholdership—especially for projects conducted on lands stewarded by Indigenous Peoples and local communities, or where these communities maintain an active relationship with the land.[5] Embedding equity into the design of carbon crediting projects—most notably land- and nature-based solutions—is essential to addressing integrity concerns and ensuring the long-term viability of interventions. When local communities are meaningfully engaged in project design, included in decision-making, and receive benefits that reflect their cultural values and community aspirations, the resulting initiatives are more likely to be contextually appropriate, credible, and sustainable.

---

3 In particular, Article 31 of the UNDRIP states that "Indigenous peoples have the right to maintain, control, protect and develop their cultural heritage, traditional knowledge and traditional cultural expressions, as well as the manifestations of their sciences, technologies and cultures, including human and genetic resources, seeds, medicines, knowledge of the properties of fauna and flora, oral traditions, literatures, designs, sports and traditional games and visual and performing arts. They also have the right to maintain, control, protect and develop their intellectual property over such cultural heritage, traditional knowledge, and traditional cultural expressions." While the UNDRIP is a declaration, not a treaty, and therefore not legally binding in the same way, it enjoys significant international support, with 143 jurisdictions voting in favor of the declaration, and Australia, Canada, New Zealand, and the United States later reversing their initial rejections.

4 K. Hamrick, K. Myers, and A. Soewito. 2023. *Beyond Beneficiaries: Fairer Carbon Market Frameworks*. The Nature Conservancy. p. 20.

5 Climate Collective. 2024. Indigenous Shareholder-ship in Environmental Markets: A Non-Exhaustive Analysis of Indigenous Peoples' Participation and Challenges in Carbon and Nature Markets.

Figure 17: Approaches to Benefit-Sharing and Engagement with Indigenous Peoples and Local Communities

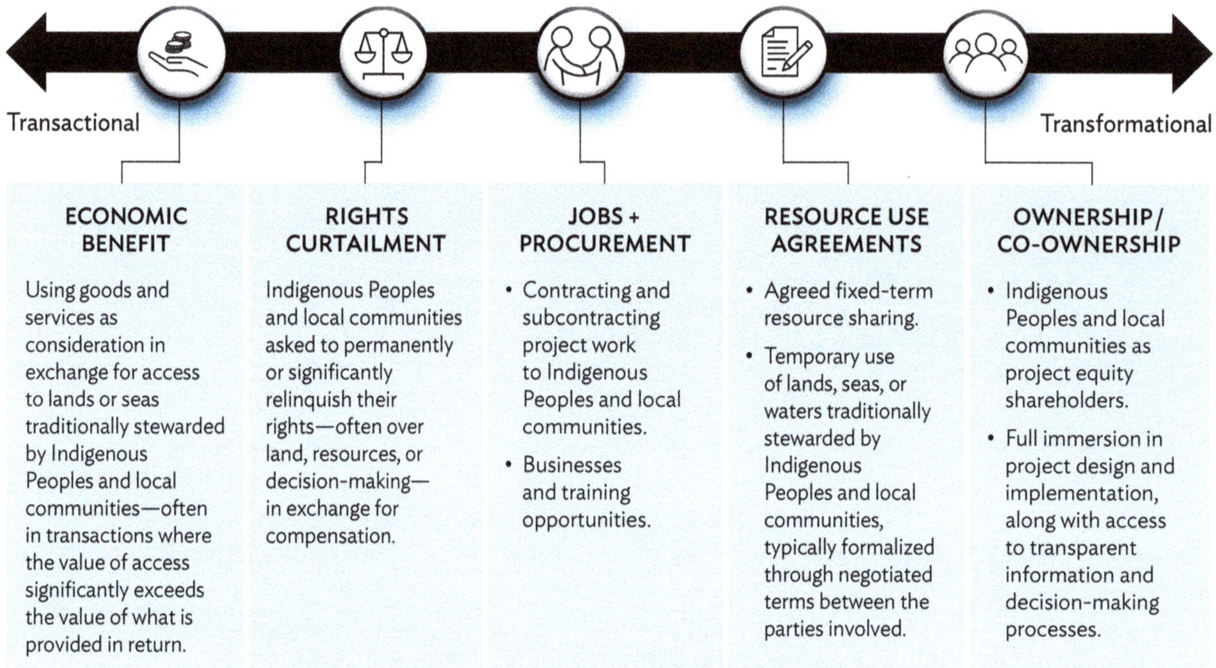

Source: Figure developed for this blueprint by the Asian Development Bank and Pollination.

How equity manifests in project design will vary based on the local context, with specific arrangements to be negotiated among the parties involved in each carbon crediting project. However, ADB DMCs should remain mindful of the power imbalances that can exist between Indigenous Peoples and local communities and project proponents or other interested parties. Regulatory frameworks should aim to reframe the prevailing model—from one centered on consultation and consent—to one that recognizes Indigenous Peoples and local communities as shareholders, partners, and preferably, leaders in carbon crediting projects.

In this context, ADB DMCs may wish to include in their legal frameworks specific requirements or incentives for projects to adopt transformational models, particularly those that involve ownership, co-ownership, or robust and meaningful partnerships among project participants. For example, ADB DMCs could require project proponents to submit a project partnership plan, developed through a process grounded in FPIC, that reflects input from all project participants and those impacted by the project, including land rights holders, Indigenous stewards, local communities, women, and minority groups. It should clearly identify all involved parties, outline a mechanism for equitable governance and decision-making, and specify the nature and distribution methods of any benefits (monetary or nonmonetary).

Some countries have also adopted regulatory provisions that state a specific percentage of carbon credit revenues to be shared with specific participants, depending on the type of land on which the project is implemented. While this represents a more prescriptive approach, ADB DMCs should ensure that any such measures reflect the genuine objectives and aspirations of the communities involved.

Additionally, strengthening local land tenure systems could be considered as part of a broader suite of social safeguards to enable Indigenous Peoples and local communities to make decisions over, and benefit from, carbon crediting projects on their land.

Ultimately, the development of legislative provisions in this area will depend heavily on the specific domestic context of each ADB DMC. Relevant considerations include whether any Indigenous Peoples or local communities may be directly or indirectly affected by carbon crediting projects; their objectives in engaging with carbon markets; and the presence—or absence—of existing mechanisms that protect, respect, and uphold their rights. The design of such provisions should be developed through meaningful and sustained consultation with Indigenous Peoples and local communities at the local, regional, and national levels, ensuring their leadership and active involvement throughout the process.

INTERNATIONAL EXAMPLE

In 2024, Brazil enacted Law 15.042, establishing a legal framework for carbon markets that includes specific provisions for carbon credits generated in areas traditionally occupied by Indigenous Peoples and "traditional peoples and communities." The law provides that "[I]ndigenous peoples and traditional peoples and communities, through their representative entities in their respective territories, and those settled in agrarian reform projects, are guaranteed the right to commercialize...carbon credits generated based on the development of projects in the territories they traditionally occupy."

For Indigenous Peoples and traditional peoples and communities, the law requires that consent be obtained through a process of free, prior, and informed consultation, as set out in International Labour Organization Convention No. 169. This consultation must respect any consultation protocols or plans adopted by the community, and the entire cost of the consultation must be covered by the project proponent, not the community. The process must also involve the Ministry of Indigenous Peoples, the National Foundation for Indigenous Peoples, and the Thematic Chamber for Indigenous Populations and Traditional Communities (within the 6th Coordination and Review Chamber of the Federal Public Prosecutor's Office), who are tasked with participating in and supervising the consultation process.

The law further requires that agreements between project proponents and Indigenous or traditional communities include a contractual clause guaranteeing fair and equitable benefit-sharing, as well as participatory management of the monetary benefits resulting from the commercialization of carbon credits through projects developed on the lands they traditionally occupy. These benefits must be deposited into a designated account and must include, at minimum, 50% of the carbon credits generated from general carbon crediting projects and 70% of those generated from REDD+ projects.

Beyond benefit-sharing, project proponents must also provide support for sustainable productive activities, social protection, cultural recognition, and territorial and environmental management. This support must align with Brazil's national policies, including the National Policy for Territorial and Environmental Management of Indigenous Lands, the National Policy for the Sustainable Development of Traditional Peoples and Communities, and the National Agrarian Reform Policy.

Finally, all agreements must contain a provision to compensate "indigenous communities, traditional peoples and communities and those settled in agrarian reform projects" for any collective, material, or immaterial damages resulting from carbon crediting projects.[a]

REDD+ = reducing emissions from deforestation and degradation and the role of conservation, sustainable management of forests, and enhancement of forest carbon stocks in developing countries.

[a] Government of Brazil. 2024. Law 15.042. Article 47. Translated from Portuguese to English using Google Translate.

Source: Asian Development Bank and Pollination.

Row of young trees. Afforestation and reforestation help restore degraded ecosystems while also creating long-term carbon sinks. By removing carbon dioxide from the atmosphere, afforestation and reforestation projects can generate carbon credits—positioning them as vital nature-based solutions within the global carbon market (photo by Gerhard Joren/ADB).

CHAPTER 7

MONITORING AND ENFORCEMENT

Monitoring, reporting, and verification (MRV) measures are crucial to ensuring the integrity of a carbon crediting scheme by confirming that emissions reductions or removals are real and measurable.

Monitoring refers to the ongoing tracking of a project's implementation and performance by the project proponents as the project progresses. This is typically carried out in accordance with the rules set by a carbon crediting standard and its associated methodology.

Reporting refers to the documentation that project proponents are required to submit, detailing the status and progress of their projects, including the amount of carbon stored or reduced as a result of project activities. These reports are generally based on the monitoring conducted during the relevant reporting period.

Verification involves the independent review and certification of the project proponent's report, including the validation of the reported emissions reductions or removals.

Enforcement refers to the mechanisms established within a domestic legal system to ensure compliance with applicable rules. ADB DMCs may employ a range of enforcement tools, which should be complemented by broader oversight and review mechanisms to facilitate transparency, accountability, and the overall integrity of the carbon crediting framework.

Figure 18 outlines the recommended building blocks and constituent elements for monitoring and enforcement provisions.

Figure 18: Monitoring and Enforcement—Building Blocks and Constituent Elements

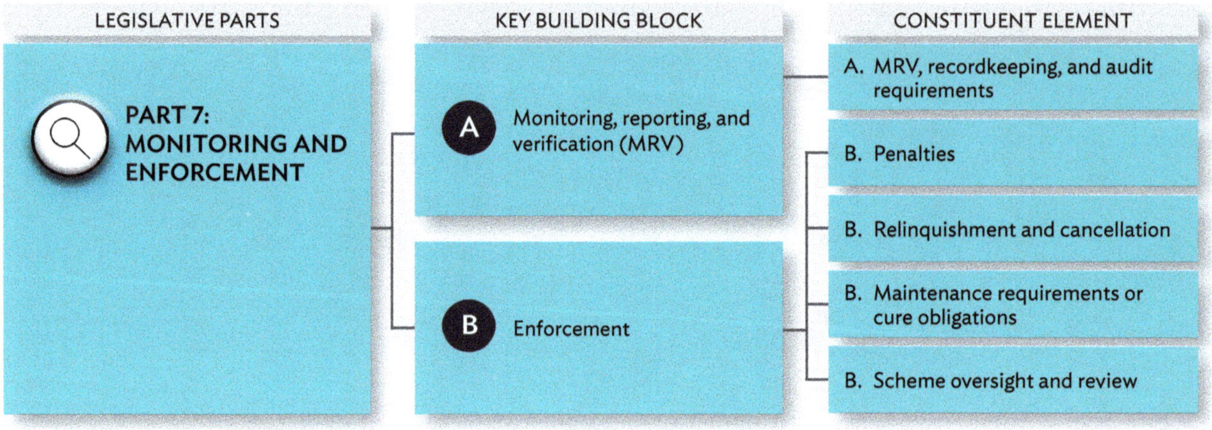

Source: Figure developed for this blueprint by the Asian Development Bank and Pollination.

7.1 Summary of Fundamental Building Blocks Likely to Be Required

Table 11 summarizes the fundamental building blocks likely to be required for MRV and enforcement provisions in ADB DMCs, with building blocks related to domestic carbon crediting schemes shown on the left, and those related to international carbon crediting standards on the right.

Table 11: Monitoring and Enforcement—Fundamental Building Blocks Likely to Be Required

FUNDAMENTAL BUILDING BLOCKS LIKELY TO BE REQUIRED	
ADB DMC Establishing a Domestic Carbon Crediting Scheme	**ADB DMC Utilizing International Carbon Crediting Standards**
✓ MRV, recordkeeping, and audit requirements.	✗ MRV requirements are not necessary, as the scheme administrator of the international carbon crediting scheme usually oversees these processes. ? However, ADB DMCs may wish to include provisions allowing domestic authorities to request information reported to the international scheme administrator (including, for example, verification reports), in order to enable domestic oversight of projects and maintain or update a national information registry, if one is established. ? ADB DMCs may also consider including provisions that allow domestic authorities to audit carbon crediting projects where there is a reasonable basis to believe the project is not complying with domestic legislation or regulations.

continued on next page

Table 11 *continued*

FUNDAMENTAL BUILDING BLOCKS LIKELY TO BE REQUIRED	
ADB DMC Establishing a Domestic Carbon Crediting Scheme	**ADB DMC Utilizing International Carbon Crediting Standards**
✓ Enforcement measures, which may include a range of penalties such as revocation of project approval, requirements to relinquish or cancel a specified number of carbon credits, or obligations to maintain emissions reductions or removals.	✓ While international carbon crediting standards typically include some enforcement mechanisms—such as the ability to de-register a project from the scheme—they may not have the same power to oversee and enforce integrity or other jurisdiction-specific requirements. They also may not be able to impose fines or sanctions on project proponents that breach the rules of the scheme. Therefore, ADB DMCs should still consider including enforcement provisions, which may include a range of penalties, such as revocation of project approval, requirements to relinquish or cancel a certain number of carbon credits, and obligations to maintain emissions reductions or removals.
✓ Scheme oversight and review mechanisms, which can be integrated into the governance framework discussed in Part B, Chapter 2: Governance of this blueprint. These mechanisms may include public consultations, periodic reviews, and grievance processes to enable participants and stakeholders to provide feedback.	✗ Scheme oversight and review mechanisms are not required, as these are typically built into the governance framework of international carbon crediting schemes. ? However, ADB DMCs should ensure that any legislation—along with associated regulations, rules, or guidelines—is adopted in line with public and administrative law requirements, including provisions for public consultation and access to grievance mechanisms where applicable.

ADB = Asian Development Bank; DMC = developing member country; MRV = monitoring, reporting, and verification.

Legend: ✓ likely to be required.
? not likely to be required but with details for determination.
✗ not likely to be required.

Source: ADB and Pollination.

7.2 Key Building Block A: Monitoring, Reporting, and Verification

MRV processes help ensure that emissions reductions or removals are real and are being generated as described in project documentation. These processes are typically defined by international carbon crediting standards and their associated methodologies. However, ADB DMCs that choose to rely on international schemes may still wish to include additional MRV provisions to strengthen the integrity of carbon credits generated domestically.

For ADB DMCs that intend to develop their own domestic carbon crediting schemes, it will be essential to incorporate clear MRV requirements into the legal framework governing carbon crediting projects implemented within their jurisdictions.

7.2.1 Monitoring, Reporting, Verification, Recordkeeping, and Audit Requirements

ADB DMCs may consider the following MRV and audit requirements.

Monitoring and Reporting

(i) Require project proponents to collect data and report on emissions reductions or removals achieved within a specified reporting period to the scheme administrator;

(ii) Establish and implement quality management procedures to ensure accurate handling of data and information; and

(iii) Require continuous monitoring by project proponents throughout the life of the project.

When setting monitoring requirements and procedures, ADB DMCs establishing their own domestic carbon crediting schemes must carefully balance flexibility—accommodating diverse project types and designs—with the need for standardization to ensure consistency, comparability, and the environmental integrity of the credits generated. Standardization is crucial for effective regulatory oversight across different project types. It also supports integrity in credit issuance by providing a common set of metrics and data points as the basis for issuing credits.

In determining project reporting frequency, ADB DMCs must balance providing project proponents with flexibility suited to their specific project design against the scheme administrator's need for sufficient oversight. Reporting intervals may vary by project type; for example, sequestration projects often require longer periods to produce measurable emissions removals, making longer reporting intervals appropriate.

Recognizing that project monitoring can be costly for certain project types, ADB DMCs may consider policy measures to alleviate these expenses. Such measures could include offering incentives—like allowing a portion of monitoring costs to be tax-deductible—at least until new technologies emerge that reduce monitoring costs.

INTERNATIONAL EXAMPLE

In many jurisdictions (e.g., Australia, Fiji, Indonesia, and New Zealand), project proponents are responsible for monitoring their own projects, subject to specific requirements regarding what must be monitored. In Australia, for instance, monitoring requirements are typically outlined in the applicable methodology, and project proponents are required to submit a report to the regulator for each designated reporting period.[a]

[a] Government of Australia. *Carbon Credits (Carbon Farming Initiative) Act 2011 (Cth)*. Sections 76 and 194.

Source: Asian Development Bank and Pollination.

Verification

Independent verification is essential to maintaining the integrity of carbon crediting schemes but can also be resource-intensive. ADB DMCs should consider requiring that reported emissions reductions or removals undergo independent verification. This process could be carried out by an independent auditor certified under a recognized emissions reduction standard, or by another entity with the necessary technical expertise required by the government. ADB DMCs may also choose to require that verification complies with international best practices or standards.

For DMCs with limited resources or technical capacity, it may be more practical to require project proponents to engage their own verifiers. However, this approach can give rise to conflicts of interest, and appropriate safeguards should be established to mitigate this risk. For example, project proponents could be required to engage only validation and verification bodies that are qualified under an existing independent standard or approved under a verification framework established by the ADB DMC.

INTERNATIONAL EXAMPLE

In the Bahamas, all emissions reductions must be carefully recorded and documented for every offset scheme, using appropriate accounting methods, corresponding adjustments, and location-specific data as required by the UNFCCC and other relevant standard-setting bodies. The Bahamas also prohibits the trading of carbon offsets unless each project is validated by a reliable and independent auditor prior to its commencement and each outcome is subsequently verified.[a]

In Indonesia, project proponents are required to engage independent third parties for project validation and verification.[b] These entities must be accredited by the National Accreditation Committee, demonstrate competence in the context of Indonesia's carbon market framework, and have no conflict of interest—whether direct or indirect—in the implementation of carbon crediting projects.[c]

By contrast, Tanzania, which regulates the use of independent standards, requires that project verification be carried out in accordance with the rules and procedures of the applicable independent carbon crediting standard.[d]

UNFCCC = United Nations Framework Convention on Climate Change.

[a] Government of the Bahamas. 2022. *Climate Change and Carbon Market Initiatives Act, 2022*. Section 13.

[b] Government of Indonesia. 2022. *Regulation of the Minister of Environment and Forestry No. 21 of 2022: Procedure for Implementation of Carbon Pricing*. Articles 14 and 16.

[c] Footnote b, Article 40.

[d] Government of Tanzania. 2022. *Environmental Management (Control and Management of Carbon Trading Regulations) 2022*. Regulation 32.

Source: Asian Development Bank and Pollination.

Recordkeeping

To facilitate transparency, ADB DMCs should require project proponents to retain project-related records for a defined period.

Clear recordkeeping requirements can strengthen enforcement and oversight efforts by ensuring that key project information remains available for audit and review. When determining the appropriate retention period, ADB DMCs should consider:

(i) the time frame within which enforcement actions may be initiated (e.g., when an audit might be ordered);

(ii) any applicable recordkeeping or auditing obligations under other legislation or general law; and

(iii) the administrative burden placed on project proponents.

Recordkeeping requirements and time frames adopted in Australia and New Zealand are given in the following example.

INTERNATIONAL EXAMPLE

In Australia, project proponents are required to maintain records of certain information related to their projects in a form that is readily accessible for inspection and audit. These records must be retained for 7 years from the date they are created. The types of information that are required to be recorded and preserved include, but are not limited to: (i) correspondence between the proponent and the regulator relevant to the project; (ii) information substantiating any declarations made by the proponent; (iii) project reports; (iv) audit reports issued in relation to the project; (v) data collected through project monitoring activities; (vi) information on any event that is reasonably likely to significantly affect the level of carbon abatement resulting from the project; and (vii) for sequestration offset projects, explanations for any carbon abatement during a reporting period that did not qualify as eligible carbon abatement.[a]

In New Zealand, project proponents must keep sufficient records to enable the Environmental Protection Authority to verify, for any given year in which an activity was carried out, the nature of the activities, the emissions removals resulting from those activities, and the proponent's entitlement to receive New Zealand Units. If the records relate to forestry activities, they must be retained for at least 20 years following the end of the year to which they relate. For all other activities, the retention period is at least 7 years from the end of the relevant year.[b]

[a] Government of Australia. *Carbon Credits (Carbon Farming Initiative) Act 2011 (Cth)*, Section 191; and Government of Australia. 2011 (updated 2024). *Carbon Credits (Carbon Farming Initiative) Rule 2015*. Rules 100 and 101.

[b] Government of New Zealand. 2002. *Climate Change Response Act 2002*. Section 67.

Source: Asian Development Bank and Pollination.

Audit

Audit requirements should be established to assess a project proponent's compliance with provisions governing carbon crediting projects. Audits may be conducted on a random basis or targeted where the scheme administrator has reasonable grounds to suspect a breach of legal requirements.

REDD+ Considerations

ADB DMCs with existing or planned national REDD+ programs will need to consider how to implement MRV at the jurisdictional scale. This involves establishing appropriate institutional arrangements—including MRV methodologies and tools, forest policies and governance structures, and national MRV systems—alongside the technical capacity to measure, report, and verify greenhouse gas (GHG) emissions reductions or removals from site-scale REDD+ projects. These

DMCs should also consider how site-scale activities will be integrated into—or "nested" within—the broader jurisdictional program.

Article 6 Reporting Considerations

ADB DMCs that are parties to the Paris Agreement will have reporting obligations under Article 6. Meeting these obligations will depend on the DMC's ability to access accurate information and data on domestic mitigation activities, including those implemented through carbon crediting projects. As such, ADB DMCs should consider how the design of their domestic legal frameworks, including any MRV requirements imposed on project developers, can support compliance with these obligations. This may include, for example, establishing a national registry to track and report on carbon crediting projects undertaken in the country and their outcomes.[1]

7.3 Key Building Block B: Enforcement

Enforcement provisions play a critical role in ensuring the effective functioning of domestic carbon crediting activities. They help ensure that project proponents adhere to legal requirements, whether projects are developed under domestic schemes or domestically approved international carbon crediting schemes.

ADB DMCs should consider tailoring enforcement provisions to their national circumstances. This involves reviewing domestic laws and frameworks to determine how they can be adapted or integrated into the carbon market legal framework. ADB DMCs can consider a range of enforcement options, from warnings or minor financial penalties for less serious infractions, to more substantive actions such as credit relinquishment or carbon maintenance orders in cases of carbon reversals.

Even when international carbon crediting standards are used, effective domestic oversight and enforcement mechanisms remain essential for ADB DMCs, because international scheme administrators may lack the legal authority to enforce integrity requirements or impose penalties on project proponents operating within a specific jurisdiction. Many projects are approved by these administrators based on representations made by project proponents that they will comply with applicable rules and methodologies. If existing domestic laws on fraud do not adequately address misconduct in carbon markets, ADB DMCs should consider incorporating specific enforcement provisions to address fraudulent conduct.

Special consideration may also be necessary for ADB DMCs seeking to participate in—or facilitate activity participants to participate in—the Paris Agreement Crediting Mechanism (PACM). Under PACM standards, host parties may withdraw project approval or authorization of activity participants.[2] This authority could serve as one of several enforcement mechanisms in an ADB DMC's "toolbox," either as an alternative to or in conjunction with other enforcement mechanisms described below in *Part B, Chapter 7: Monitoring and Enforcement, Section 7.3.1—Project-Level Enforcement Mechanisms* of this blueprint.

1 See *Part B, Chapter 5: Article 6 Requirements, Section 5.5—Key Building Block D: Reporting* of this blueprint.

2 UNFCCC. A6.4-PROC-AC-002. Part 11, paras. 220–224.

ADB DMCs should also determine which entity will be responsible for monitoring and enforcement. Typically, this is the agency tasked with administering the relevant legal framework, such as an independent regulator (if established) or a designated government department. The choice of entity should reflect both the legal and institutional structure of the country and the technical capacity of the relevant body. More serious enforcement actions, such as those involving criminal penalties, may require involvement of other government departments or the judiciary. In designing enforcement roles and responsibilities, ADB DMCs should also ensure compliance with applicable administrative and public law requirements within their jurisdiction.

7.3.1 Project-Level Enforcement Mechanisms

7.3.1.1 Penalties

Penalties are an important enforcement tool and can serve as a deterrent to participants who might otherwise contravene domestic laws and regulations on carbon crediting. ADB DMCs could consider classifying certain behaviors, such as knowingly providing false or misleading information to the relevant regulatory body or registry, as offenses that may attract criminal liability or administrative penalties. These penalties could include monetary fines, suspension of credit issuance, project deregistration, and/or temporary suspension from participation in the scheme.

INTERNATIONAL EXAMPLE

In many jurisdictions (particularly common law jurisdictions such as Australia, Fiji, and New Zealand), penalties may only be enforced by a court of law following a formal determination regarding the conduct of the project proponent or the project's compliance with relevant legislative requirements.

Source: Asian Development Bank and Pollination.

7.3.1.2 Revocation of Project Approval or Registration

ADB DMCs could consider including provisions in their legal frameworks to suspend and, where appropriate, revoke the approval or registration of carbon crediting projects. This could apply to projects registered under either an international carbon crediting standard—where the DMC would revoke its approval for the project to operate within its jurisdiction—or under the DMC's own domestic carbon crediting program.

Suspension or revocation may be warranted in circumstances such as:

(i) the project has failed to obtain required regulatory approvals,
(ii) the project no longer meets the eligibility requirements set out in the legal framework, or
(iii) the project proponent is found to have submitted false or misleading information during the approval or registration process.

Given the significant impact these measures can have on project proponents, ADB DMCs should also include procedural safeguards. For example, the legal framework could require the enforcement body to notify the proponent of its intention to suspend or revoke approval and provide an opportunity to respond or remedy the identified issues before suspension or revocation takes effect.

If approval is revoked for a project registered under an international carbon crediting standard, the ADB DMC would also need to coordinate with the carbon crediting program administrator to ensure that the project is formally deregistered from the relevant registry.

In addition, ADB DMCs that include revocation provisions should consider the implications for carbon credits already issued. In some cases, the reason for revocation—such as noncompliance with the applicable methodology—may affect the validity of the credits themselves and result in over-crediting.[3] The DMC may therefore need to consider whether any issued credits should also be cancelled or invalidated. This issue is relevant only where the DMC operates its own domestic carbon crediting program, as the issuance and revocation of credits under international carbon crediting programs are managed by the relevant scheme administrator in accordance with program rules.

7.3.1.3 Relinquishment

To ensure accountability and integrity, ADB DMCs could consider requiring project proponents to relinquish a specified number of carbon credits as a penalty in certain circumstances, including:

(i) where the project proponent has provided false or misleading information, or has committed fraud related to the issuance of carbon credits;

(ii) where the project's approval or registration has been revoked (e.g., due to noncompliance with the legal framework or applicable standard); or

(iii) where there has been a complete or partial reversal of the mitigation outcomes generated by the project. Typically, this requirement would exclude reversals caused by natural disasters or other events beyond the proponent's control, where the proponent has taken reasonable preventative measures. Such cases are generally addressed through buffer pool mechanisms or credit issuance discounts.

Relinquishment differs from revocation.[4] Relinquishment involves a requirement imposed on the project proponent to cancel credits equivalent to those affected. These may be the affected credits themselves (if still held by the proponent) or equivalent replacement credits.

On the other hand, revocation refers to the cancellation of affected credits by the scheme administrator, regardless of current ownership (e.g., if held by a third-party purchaser). It could be used where there are issues with the issuance of the credits, such as over-crediting. In these instances, any market impact from the cancellation must be managed through private contractual arrangements, such as damages or replacement credits, particularly where the revocation results from the proponent's fault.

ADB DMCs could also require that failure to comply with a relinquishment notice may result in the imposition of a monetary penalty.

---

3 Over-crediting means some of the credits issued do not actually represent verified emissions reductions or removals. See *Part B, Chapter 4: Carbon Credits, Section 4.2.1—Process for Issuing Credits* and *Part B, Chapter 7: Monitoring and Enforcement, Section 7.3.1.3—Relinquishment* of this blueprint for further details.

4 See *Part B, Chapter 4: Carbon Credits, Section 4.2.1—Process for Issuing Credits* of this blueprint.

7.3.1.4 Maintenance Requirements or Cure Obligations

In some instances, the project proponent may be required to cure a project, such as when a carbon reversal has occurred due to the proponent's fault. An obligation to maintain or cure may include, for example, legal orders prohibiting actions that would likely result in the loss or reduction of sequestered carbon, as well as requirements for the proponent to take all reasonable steps to rectify any reversal or diminution that has occurred. For instance, they may be required to regrow vegetation or to actively re-establish carbon stores, depending on the applicable project methodology.

Where appropriate, these legal obligations could also attach to the land itself—for instance, through registration on land titles—thereby extending cure requirements to landowners or occupiers, even if they are not the project proponents. Given the gravity and potentially serious implications of these measures, especially for landowners and local communities who may not be operationally responsible for project implementation, ADB DMCs may need to integrate free, prior and informed consent (FPIC) considerations into the design and application of such requirements.

7.3.2 Scheme Oversight and Review Mechanisms

While project-level enforcement mechanisms are important, they should be complemented by a scheme design that enables the carbon crediting scheme administrator to maintain continuous project oversight. This oversight should allow for early identification of noncompliance and offer stakeholders and affected parties an opportunity to raise concerns or report issues (Figure 19).

Figure 19: Scheme Oversight and Review Mechanisms

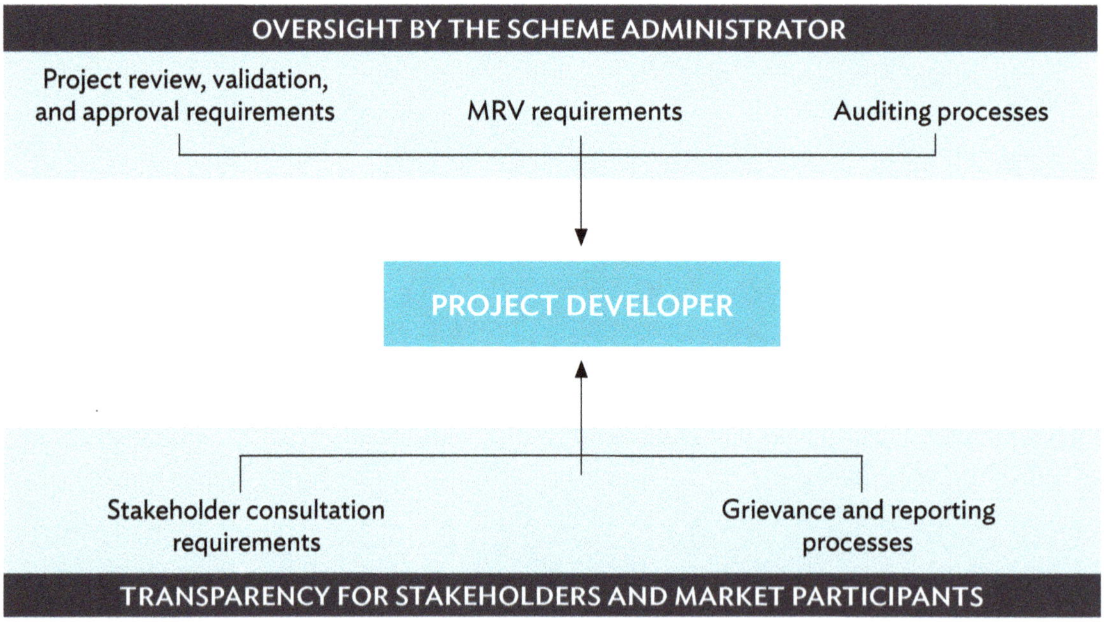

MRV = monitoring, reporting, and verification.
Source: Figure developed for this blueprint by the Asian Development Bank and Pollination.

Solar panels convert sunlight into electricity. In Asia and the Pacific, rapid growth in solar installations supports rural electrification, growing urban energy demands, and national climate goals. Countries such as the People's Republic of China, India, and Viet Nam are leading large-scale solar development, while Pacific island nations use solar power to increase energy access and reduce reliance on imported fossil fuels (photo by Moritz Kindler/Unsplash).

A man harvests tomatoes in a climate-controlled greenhouse in Armenia. Optimizing heating, lighting, and irrigation systems within such facilities can lead to quantifiable reductions in energy consumption and associated emissions. This commitment to sustainable agriculture creates opportunities for carbon finance, as investments in these energy efficiencies can result in verifiable emission reductions that may be eligible for carbon credits (photo by Eric Sales/ADB).

APPENDIXES

Appendix 1
Minimum Requirements for Carbon Crediting Legal Frameworks

Table A1.1: Summary of Minimum Requirements for Carbon Crediting Legal Frameworks

Building Blocks and Constituent Elements	ADB DMC Establishing a Domestic Carbon Crediting Scheme	ADB DMC Utilizing International Carbon Crediting Standards
Part 1: Introductory Provisions		
Objectives and principles	✓	✓
Key definitions	✓	✓
Part 2: Governance		
Types, roles, and powers of governing bodies	✓	✓
Part 3: Carbon Crediting Projects		
Project proponent requirements	✓	✓
Process for developing and approving project methodologies	✓	?[a]
Process for approving international carbon crediting standards for use in the country	?[b]	✓
Eligibility criteria for carbon crediting projects and a process for assessing and approving projects against these criteria	✓	?[c]
Requirements for carbon crediting projects to demonstrate additionality	✓	?[d]
Requirements to ensure the permanence of emissions reductions or removals achieved by carbon crediting projects	✓	✓[e]
Requirements to mitigate the risk of double counting	✓	✓[f]
Requirements to ensure that emissions reductions and removals generated under the scheme are real, measurable, and verified	✓	✓[g]
Requirements to mitigate the risk of leakage	✓	✗
Part 4: Carbon Credits		
Process for issuing carbon credits	✓	✗
Registration of carbon credits through the establishment of a scheme registry	✓	?[h]
Transfer of carbon credits	✓	✓
Cancellation and retirement of carbon credits	✓	✗
Part 5: Article 6 Requirements		
Framework for authorizing ITMOs	✓	✓
Process for applying corresponding adjustments	✓	✓
Establish an Article 6-compliant tracking system	✓	✓
Responsibility and processes for preparing and submitting Article 6-related reports	✓	✓

continued on next page

Table A1.1 *continued*

Building Blocks and Constituent Elements	ADB DMC Establishing a Domestic Carbon Crediting Scheme	ADB DMC Utilizing International Carbon Crediting Standards
Part 6: Social and environmental safeguards		
Social and environmental safeguards	✓	✓[i]
Safeguards relating to Indigenous Peoples and local communities	✓	✓[j]
Part 7: Monitoring and enforcement		
MRV, recordkeeping, and audit requirements	✓	?[k]
Enforcement powers	✓	✓
Scheme oversight and review mechanisms	✓	x[l]

ADB = Asian Development Bank; DMC = developing member country; ITMO = internationally transferred mitigation outcome; MRV = monitoring, reporting, and verification.

Legend: ✓ likely to be required.
? not likely to be required but with details for determination.
x not likely to be required.

[a] ADB DMCs may choose to specify which methodologies under these schemes are approved for use within their country—for example, by maintaining a regularly updated list of pre-approved methodologies. DMCs that wish to participate in the Paris Agreement Crediting Mechanism (PACM), established under Article 6.4 of the Paris Agreement, must also put in place a process for determining which Article 6.4 activities (A6.4 activities) they will authorize and for formally notifying the Supervisory Body of those approvals.

[b] ADB DMCs may also choose to approve the use of international carbon crediting standards alongside the domestic scheme established under their national legal framework.

[c] ADB DMCs may choose to include a process for approving carbon crediting projects that allows them to apply additional integrity criteria, safeguards, and/or project requirements. These elements should be aligned with the country's national policy priorities and sustainable development goals.

[d] Requirements for additionality are not necessary, as this matter is already addressed under the international crediting standard. However, ADB DMCs intending to use international crediting standards should ensure that any standard approved for use in the country includes its own additionality requirement. Moreover—or as an alternative—ADB DMCs may include a broad provision in their laws and/or regulations stating that all approved projects must demonstrate additionality.

[e] ADB DMCs should have the ability to enforce the permanence obligation required by any international crediting standard they adopt.

[f] This is particularly critical for ADB DMCs seeking to engage in Article 6 of the Paris Agreement, and will need to be addressed in the DMC's rules governing authorization and corresponding adjustments.

[g] ADB DMCs should establish requirements to ensure that emissions reductions and removals from carbon crediting projects within their jurisdiction are real, measurable, and verified—for example, by ensuring that any international carbon crediting standards approved for use in the country include provisions that address this integrity principle.

[h] While not mandatory, it is recommended that ADB DMCs establish at least a basic informational registry to track carbon crediting projects conducted within their jurisdiction and the credits they generate. This would enhance transparency and provide the DMC with greater visibility into carbon market activities within the country.

[i] International carbon crediting schemes, including the PACM, typically incorporate safeguards within their standards. However, ADB DMCs should also consider implementing additional safeguards that reflect their specific domestic context and priorities.

[j] While international carbon crediting schemes typically include requirements for engagement with Indigenous Peoples and local communities, these requirements may not always be consistent or necessarily appropriate for the specific domestic context of an ADB DMC. Therefore, ADB DMCs should still strongly consider establishing their own safeguards relating to Indigenous Peoples and local communities. This includes protection of their rights—such as free, prior, and informed consent (FPIC)—as well as ensuring that these groups are meaningfully included as core partners in any carbon crediting project conducted on lands they steward or where they have an active presence or relationship.

[k] MRV requirements are not required, as these processes are usually overseen by the administrator of the international carbon crediting scheme. However, ADB DMCs may still wish to retain certain oversight powers. For example, they may include provisions to request information submitted to the international scheme administrator—such as verification reports—to support domestic oversight and to update the national informational registry, if one is in place. Additionally, ADB DMCs may consider including the authority to audit carbon crediting projects where there is a reasonable basis to believe that a project is not in compliance with national legislation or regulations.

[l] Scheme oversight and review mechanisms are not required, as these are typically embedded within the international carbon crediting schemes themselves. However, ADB DMCs should ensure that any legislation—as well as associated regulations, rules, or guidelines—is adopted in compliance with applicable public and administrative law. This includes adhering to requirements for public consultation and accessible grievance mechanisms.

Source: Asian Development Bank and Pollination.

Appendix 2
Introduction to Carbon Markets

1. What Is Carbon?

Carbon dioxide is one of several greenhouse gases (GHGs) that contribute to climate change, along with methane, hydrofluorocarbons, and nitrous oxide .

Carbon can be stored in various reservoirs across natural landscapes—such as the biomass of trees, shrubs, and other plants, as well as oceans and soils. Carbon can also be stored by technological means. When undisturbed, these reservoirs act as carbon "sinks," effectively sequestering carbon and helping mitigate GHG emissions. However, disruptions—for instance, deforestation or the extraction and combustion of fossil fuels—release the stored carbon into the atmosphere as a GHG, directly contributing to climate change.

The release and absorption of carbon is part of a continuous process called the carbon life cycle, illustrated in Figure A2.1. Within this cycle, carbon constantly moves among the various reservoirs (oceans, soils, living organisms such as plants and animals, and geological formations that contain fossil fuels). Carbon is then released into the atmosphere primarily through processes like the decay

Figure A2.1: The Carbon Life Cycle

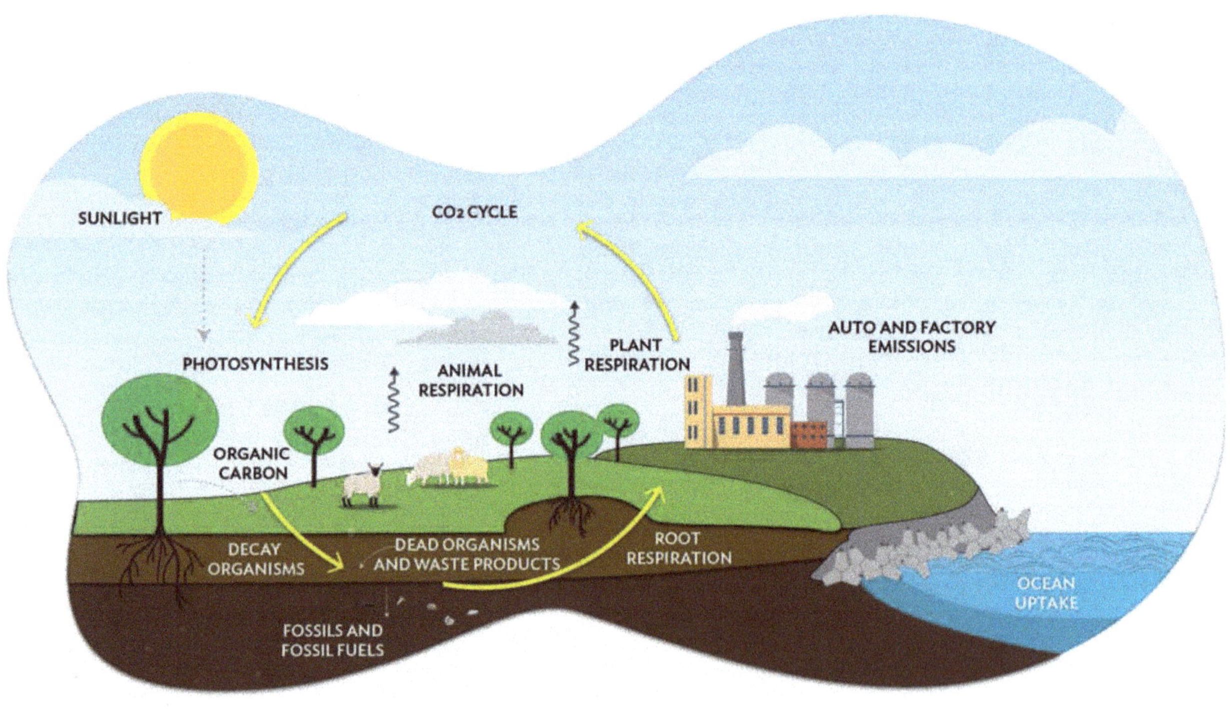

CO_2 = carbon dioxide.
Source: Concept by Pollination and rendering by Joycelyn B. Lucena/Asian Development Bank.

of organic matter, plant and animal respiration, and combustion of fossil fuels (e.g., auto and factory emissions). This atmospheric carbon dioxide is then reabsorbed by the oceans, soils, and plants and the animals that consume them, continuing the cycle.

Carbon credits and carbon markets were developed to facilitate the transition to net-zero—where GHG gas emissions are balanced with removals so that there is no impact on the climate system—by allowing carbon crediting project proponents to generate revenue from activities that reduce GHG emissions or remove or store carbon from the atmosphere.

2. What Are Carbon Markets?

Carbon markets are a trading system through which carbon credits are bought and sold.

2.1 What Are Carbon Credits?

Carbon credits are generated through activities that either remove carbon from, or reduce the amount of carbon released into, the atmosphere. Projects can generate carbon credits for every metric ton that is reduced or removed (sequestered) (Figure A2.2).

Figure A2.2: Nature of a Carbon Credit

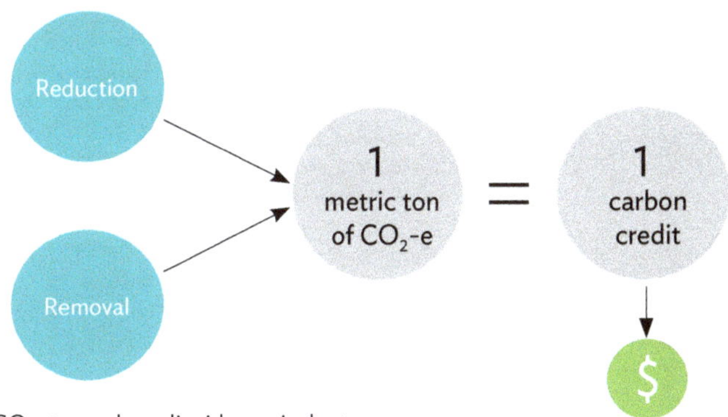

CO_2-e = carbon dioxide equivalent.
Source: Figure developed for this blueprint by the Asian Development Bank and Pollination.

2.2 How Are Carbon Credits Traded to Create a "Market"?

Carbon credits are tradable assets that can be sold to governments and businesses on various markets, enabling carbon crediting project proponents to generate revenue from activities that reduce or remove GHG emissions.

These markets are often referred to as "voluntary" or "compliance" carbon markets (Table A2.1).

Table A2.1: Voluntary Versus Compliance Carbon Markets

Voluntary Carbon Markets	Compliance Carbon Markets
VCMs "encompass [the] collection of standard bodies, voluntary buyers, and carbon credit generators that sell verified carbon credits to be used for voluntary purposes."[a] "Voluntary purposes" refers to carbon emitters, primarily corporates, purchasing carbon credits through the VCM in relation to their emissions.	Compliance carbon markets refer to domestic or international markets where an entity purchases carbon credits for compliance purposes, e.g., to help the entity meet a compulsory emissions reduction target. Carbon credits used for compliance purposes will generally need to conform to the rules of the relevant compliance regime.

VCM = voluntary carbon market.
[a] ADB. 2024. *Asia Pacific Climate Report: Catalyzing Finance and Policy Solutions*. p. 153.
Source: Asian Development Bank and Pollination.

3. Who Operates in These Markets?

Stakeholders in carbon markets operate on both the "supply side" (i.e., generating and selling carbon credits) and the "demand side" (i.e., purchasing carbon credits) (Figure A2.3). These stakeholders each have their own motivations for engaging in carbon markets, which can influence how the market functions within a country. It is therefore important to consider a broad range of stakeholders when developing laws and regulations governing carbon markets.

Figure A2.3: Key Participants in Carbon Markets

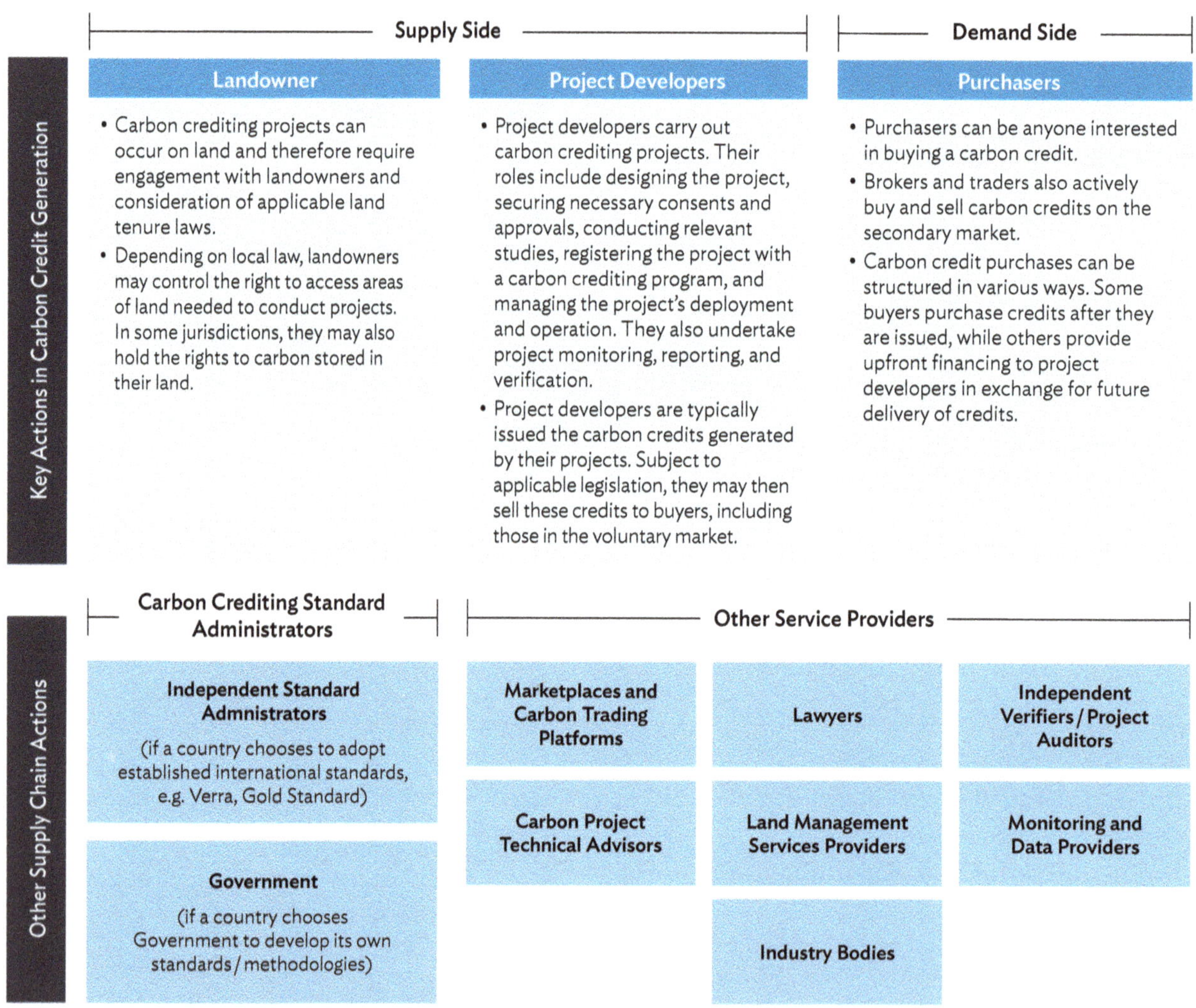

Source: Figure developed for this blueprint by the Asian Development Bank and Pollination.

Beyond direct participants and stakeholders, various global organizations work to support carbon market engagement. Their efforts include strengthening integrity frameworks and identifying opportunities to harmonize legal approaches to carbon markets. Table A2.2 summarizes the key international forums involved in these initiatives.

Table A2.2: Key International Forums Supporting Carbon Market Development and Integrity

THE INTERNATIONAL EMISSIONS TRADING ASSOCIATION (IETA)	INTERNATIONAL INSTITUTE FOR THE UNIFICATION OF PRIVATE LAW (UNIDROIT)
IETA is a "non-profit organization representing businesses committed to well-designed and effective carbon markets to help achieve the goals of the Paris Agreement and reach net-zero emissions by 2050."[a] IETA has published several papers on carbon markets, including carbon market business briefs and a carbon market readiness training guide.[b] IETA has also published model documents commonly used in various carbon market transactions.	UNIDROIT is an independent intergovernmental organization whose "purpose is to study needs and methods for modernizing, harmonizing and coordinating private and, in particular, commercial law as between States and groups of States and to formulate uniform law instruments, principles, and rules to achieve those objectives."[c] UNIDROIT, in collaboration with the World Bank Group, has launched a project to examine the legal nature of voluntary carbon credits. The initiative aims to develop an international instrument that defines and clarifies their legal status.
INTERNATIONAL ORGANIZATION OF SECURITIES COMMISSIONS (IOSCO)	**INTERNATIONAL SWAPS AND DERIVATIVES ASSOCIATION (ISDA)**
IOSCO is "the international body that brings together the world's securities regulators and is recognized as the global standard setter for the securities sector. It develops, implements, and promotes adherence to internationally recognized standards for securities regulation."[d] IOSCO has released a discussion report examining the key characteristics of robust and efficient voluntary carbon markets (VCMs), as well as the potential role of financial regulators in ensuring their integrity.[e]	ISDA's work "in developing the ISDA Master Agreement and a wide range of related documentation materials, and in ensuring the enforceability of their netting and collateral provisions, has helped to significantly reduce credit and legal risk [of securities]."[f] ISDA has published several papers on important topics related to voluntary carbon markets, including the legal implications of voluntary carbon credits,[g] definitions for carbon credit transactions,[h] and the regulatory oversight of voluntary carbon markets in the United States.[i]
INTEGRITY COUNCIL FOR THE VOLUNTARY CARBON MARKET (ICVCM)	**THE VOLUNTARY CARBON MARKETS INTEGRITY INITIATIVE (VCMI)**
The Integrity Council for the Voluntary Carbon Market is an independent governance body that focuses on ensuring supply-side integrity within the voluntary carbon market.[j]	The VCMI supports the development of high-integrity voluntary carbon markets, with a particular focus on demand-side integrity. It has released several publications on this topic, including guidance on aligning voluntary carbon market use with net zero commitments and the "VCMI Claims Code of Practice."[k]

a ERM. 2024. Sustainability Report. p. 105.
b IETA. Carbon Market Business Briefs; IETA. 2017. Carbon Market Readiness Training Guide.
c International Institute for the Unification of Private Law (UNIDROIT). 2006. Uniform Law.
d World Economic Forum. International Organization of Securities Commission.
e OICU-IOSCO. 2022. Voluntary Carbon Markets: Discussion Paper.
f ISDA. About ISDA.
g ISDA. 2021. Legal Implications of Voluntary Carbon Credits.
h ISDA. 2024. ISDA Verified Carbon Credit Transactions Definitions.
i ISDA. 2022. Voluntary Carbon Markets: Analysis of Regulatory Oversight in the US.
j Carbon Market Institute. Integrity Council for Voluntary Carbon Markets (IC-VCM).
k VCMI. 2024. Claims Code of Practice.
Source: Asian Development Bank and Pollination.

Multiple international integrity standards have emerged to create greater standardization of high-integrity carbon standards, methodologies, and projects. These standards are set out in Table A2.3.

Table A2.3: International Integrity Standards

CORSIA Emissions Unit Eligibility Criteria[a]	These criteria set the eligibility standards for units that airlines may use to fulfill their international aviation emissions reduction commitments. They provide a useful reference for Asian Development Bank (ADB) developing member countries (DMCs) when designing domestic carbon crediting schemes, methodologies, or integrity criteria. Additionally, these criteria can serve as a helpful guide for evaluating international carbon crediting schemes that may be approved for use within the country.
Tropical Forest Credit Integrity Guide[b]	This guide has been developed to help companies identify high-quality forest carbon credits. It provides a set of considerations for buyers conducting due diligence on forest carbon credit projects, serving as a valuable resource for ADB DMCs on the integrity elements that buyers seek in a forest carbon crediting framework.
The Integrity Council for the Voluntary Carbon Market's Core Carbon Principles (CCPs)[c]	The CCPs are a global benchmark developed by the Integrity Council for the Voluntary Carbon Market to promote high-integrity voluntary carbon markets. They are operationalized through an "Assessment Framework," which provides detailed guidance on their implementation. The CCPs can serve as a useful reference for ADB DMCs seeking to integrate integrity elements into a domestic carbon crediting scheme. Projects or credits that meet CCP criteria are likely to attract greater market demand.
The Climate, Community and Biodiversity (CCB) Standards[d]	Administered by Verra, the CCB Standards facilitate the assessment and labeling of projects that incorporate climate, community, and biodiversity benefit approaches into their design and implementation.
United Kingdom's (UK) Department for Energy Security and Net Zero's Principles for Voluntary Carbon and Nature Market Integrity[e]	The Government of the UK has published a policy paper outlining principles to support integrity in voluntary carbon and nature markets.

[a] International Civil Aviation Organization. 2019. *CORSIA Emissions Unit Eligibility Criteria*.

[b] Conservation International, Coordination of the Indigenous Organizations of the Amazon Basin, Environmental Defense Fund, IPAM Amazônia, The Nature Conservancy, Wildlife Conservation Society, World Resources Institute, WWF. 2023. *Tropical Forest Credit Integrity Guide*.

[c] ICVCM. 2025. *Core Carbon Principles*.

[d] Verra. 2025. *Climate, Community & Biodiversity Standards*.

[e] United Kingdom's Department for Energy Security and Net Zero. 2024. *Policy Paper: Principles for Voluntary Carbon and Nature Market Integrity*. 15 November.

Source: Asian Development Bank and Pollination.

4. Carbon Credit Generation and Sale

Carbon market stakeholders interact through a range of contractual and other arrangements at different stages of the carbon crediting project process. Figure A2.4 illustrates these arrangements, detailing each stage involved in the generation and sale of carbon credits.

Figure A2.4: Indicative Stages of Carbon Credit Generation and Sale

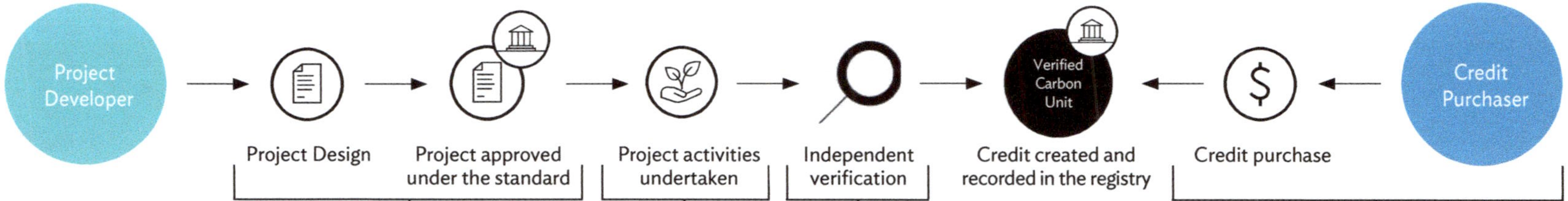

LANDOWNER / STANDARD ADMINISTRATORS · PROJECT DEVELOPER / INVESTORS/FINANCIERS	LANDOWNER · PROJECT DEVELOPER / LAND MANAGEMENT SERVICES PROVIDERS	PROJECT DEVELOPER · INDEPENDENT VERIFIERS / MONITORING AND DATA PROVIDERS	PROJECT DEVELOPER · PURCHASERS / MMARKETPLACES AND CARBON TRADING PLATFORMS
Project developers are responsible for designing the project and coordinating the necessary approvals and documentation. The **project design documentation**—defined by the rules of the relevant standard and/or its administrators—usually includes a draft project description and evidence of project ownership. At this stage, project developers generally enter into **agreements with landowners** to facilitate access, transfer carbon rights, and outline other relevant terms. They may also establish financing arrangements with third-party investors or financiers.	Project developers can carry out the project activities themselves or contract others to do so. They may enter into **agreements with specialist land management service contractors** (such as those that assist with project design and implementation), as well as with **landowners and/or local communities** to undertake these activities.	Verification is usually undertaken by an independent verification entity. Project developers enter into a **contractual agreement to engage a validation and/or verification provider**. The carbon crediting standard may require that the verifier possess specific qualifications or be selected from an accredited pool of accredited entities.	Purchasers can buy carbon credits directly by entering into agreements with project developers, such as **emissions reduction purchase agreements**. They may also use **offtake agreements**, where buyers commit to purchasing credits at predetermined prices several years into the future. Alternatively, purchasers can buy credits on the market through independent trading platforms, usually agreeing to standard sale terms and conditions when registering on such platforms and listing credits there for sale.

Source: Figure developed for this blueprint by the Asian Development Bank and Pollination.

5. What Types of Activities Are Eligible for Generating Credits?

Generally, each carbon crediting standard has a set of "methodologies" that define the types of activities eligible to be credited under the carbon crediting scheme.

Broadly, carbon crediting projects fall into two categories:

1. **Emissions reduction.** Project activities reduce the level of emissions being released into the atmosphere; and
2. **Emissions removal.** Projects that remove carbon from the atmosphere.

Projects are also referred to as either "nature-based" and "industrial" or "tech-based." This refers to the type of mitigation activity used to achieve the emissions reductions or removals.

Table A2.4 presents examples of these types of projects.

Table A2.4: Types of Carbon Credit-Generating Activities

<table>
<tr><th></th><th>Nature-Based Solutions EMISSIONS REMOVAL</th><th>Nature-Based Solutions EMISSIONS REDUCTION</th><th>Industrial or Tech-Based EMISSIONS REMOVAL</th><th>Industrial or Tech-Based EMISSIONS REDUCTION</th></tr>
<tr><td rowspan="2">EXAMPLE PROJECTS</td><td>• Afforestation/ reforestation (planting trees)</td><td>• Savanna burning activities, which reduce fuel loads through controlled burning, thereby reducing GHG emissions from larger, more intense wildfires</td><td rowspan="2">• Direct Air Capture with Carbon Storage (DACCS), which uses chemical processes to capture carbon dioxide directly from ambient air, with the captured CO_2 then stored in geological reservoirs or used to produce long-lasting products
• Bioenergy with Carbon Capture and Storage (BECCS), which involves capturing and permanently storing CO_2 from processes that convert biomass into fuels or burn it directly to generate energy</td><td rowspan="2">• Renewable energy projects, which can include activities such as replacing fossil fuel-based electricity generation with renewable sources, distributing efficient improved cooking stoves (ICS) to rural households, expanding the use of renewable-powered electric vehicle charging, and switching from emissions-intensive fuels to low-carbon alternatives
• Industrial energy efficiency upgrades</td></tr>
<tr><td colspan="2">• Blue carbon, which can include activities such as restoring tidal wetlands and preventing mangrove forest loss
• Soil carbon, which involves adopting land management practices that increase soil carbon stocks (an emissions removal activity) and reducing emissions through measures such as fertilizer reduction
• REDD+, which aims to reduce emissions from deforestation and forest degradation in developing countries, and to sequester carbon by enhancing forest carbon stocks</td></tr>
</table>

CO_2 = carbon dioxide; GHG = greenhouse gas; REDD+ = reducing emissions from deforestation and degradation and the role of conservation, sustainable management of forests, and enhancement of forest carbon stocks in developing countries.
Source: Figure developed for this blueprint by the Asian Development Bank and Pollination.

6. What About REDD+?

REDD+ stands for:

- **R**educing
- **E**missions from
- **D**eforestation and forest
- **D**egradation.
- The "**+**" in REDD+ stands for:
    - the role of conservation,
    - sustainable management of forests, and
    - enhancement of forest carbon stocks.

Developed under the United Nations Framework Convention on Climate Change (UNFCCC), REDD+ is a globally agreed framework that incentivizes national efforts to protect, conserve, and restore forest ecosystems in developing countries by valuing carbon removals, storage, and other social and environmental services. The REDD+ framework can apply to all types of forests, including mangrove forests.

REDD+ activities include:

(i) reducing emissions from deforestation,
(ii) reducing emissions from degradation,
(iii) conservation of forest carbon stocks,
(iv) enhancement of forest carbon stocks, and
(v) sustainable management of forests.

The REDD+ framework for national and subnational implementation was developed over the course of a decade. During this time, numerous project-scale REDD+ activities were developed under independent carbon crediting standards. These project-scale REDD+ activities played an important role in building local implementation capacity and generating valuable lessons.

"National REDD+ programs define measures to address deforestation, conserve and enhance forest carbon stocks, establish a forest reference emissions level, establish forest monitoring systems, and define benefit sharing and safeguards."[1] With national REDD+ programs now operational, there is growing recognition that REDD+ implementation—at any scale—must align with national accounting frameworks and incentive structures.

The process for incorporating and formally recognizing site- or subnational-scale REDD+ activities within national REDD+ programs is called "nesting."

[1] C. Streck et al. 2021. The Voluntary Carbon Market Explained. Chapter 13: How Does the Voluntary Carbon Market Incorporate REDD+? p. 1.